PAULA HART

RIDING

THE

CHANGE

NAVIGATING UNPRECEDENTED TIMES

GUIDANCE FOR HUMANITY
FROM THE FIELD OF TRUTH

Arcadia Press

Riding The Change
Navigating Unprecedented Times.
Guidance for Humanity from The Field Of Truth.

© Copyright Paula Hart 2020

All rights reserved.

Published 2020

ISBN 978-0-6483772-4-5

Published by Arcadia Press

www.arcadiapress.com.au

Country of publication: Australia

Disclaimer: This book is made available with the understanding that its contents contain the ideas and opinions of its author and contributor and that these ideas and opinions should not be construed as medical advice for any individual, their condition or life situation. The reader is also encouraged to seek the advice and support of their trusted health care professionals where required.

Contents

CHAPTER 4

Moving ahead with style 51

CHAPTER 5

Unfurling the flag...57

CHAPTER 6

Loosening the ties...61

CHAPTER 7

Completion 65

CHAPTER 8

Totality..69

Foreword

Having received my earlier book from Pleiadians, I found this one to be coming through with a different energy. Asking who was pouring this information through me, led to the following conversation:

My dear it matters not. There is only one source of Truth after all. Call it by any name you like, it comes to the same. The idea of separate entities you now know well is illusory, so why support it? You can say it originates from the Field of Truth. There is no need for personalities or identities where Truth resides. For that concept immediately taints the Truth itself. Call it God and once again you have fallen into a trap of limitation. The fact is that Truth is freely available and needs no boundaries. It is there for the taking and may be slightly shaped in its expression by the receiver, but the time for it to be labelled as from an identity is past. The Truth comes from Freedom itself.

In the past the limitations humanity placed on possibility necessitated some humouring in the realms of transmission. You needed to believe the message was from someone reputable, from one of your major religions or mythologies. Now you have grown in discrimination to the point where you can recognize a truth and do not need this small crutch. This is an aspect of your reclaiming of your power, after millennia of giving it away to authorities and limited concepts.

So indeed, the Truth you harvest comes from the Field of Truth which is infinite and available to all who seek it.

In the world of channelers this might sound like heresy at best and nonsense at worst. How then to explain the differences in content, intonation and expression of different channelings? Some via Indigenous elders, or Ascended Masters, or extraterrestrials... Are you saying then that this channelling comes from individuals rather than from the Field of unlimited Truth, and is therefore limited by the perceptions of those who impart the information?

Yes exactly.

This is why I had shelved the Pleiadian book- I felt it must be limited by the bias of the Pleiadians, even though well meant. But surely the unbiased Truth would contain very few words? What can be true apart from I Am?

That is not so. If your mission is to mine information leading to the awakening and peace of humanity there are true words to fit that aim.

I need clarity here: You have said there are no individual entities and I understand that. But then you agreed that some channelling comes via individual entities. Can you explain this contradiction please?

My dear you understand that the One plays as many. The One is the Truth, the many are a lesser truth, or one could say, an illusion. If the One could be said to perceive, that perception would be clear, devoid of biases and clouds. This is the Field of Truth. The perceptions of the many are clouded and tainted by the illusory nature of their belief in their separate existence. They could be said to be impure.

How about Ascended Masters? Have they not risen above these clouds of illusion and into the Field of Truth itself?

Each still retains remnants of the personalities it once deemed itself to be. These remnants may colour the words of these beings.

Maybe some of those beings who are channelled access the Field of Truth itself? E.g. some American Indians, some Ascended Masters..?

Indeed, some do. And some do not, but rather speak of their own wisdoms, gleaned from lessons learned in their lifetimes.

I suppose really the important thing is for the reader to notice what resonates deeply and what does not.

That is it. Each person will resonate to the truth they are ready to receive.

How can anyone, including me, hear the words from the Field of Truth accurately and without tainting them with our own biased perceptions?

With great difficulty. It takes discrimination as well as determination to "get it right". Your use of dowsing helps you check your accuracy of reception and others have other means, while some do indeed receive a perverted version.

Now this next book, Riding the Change, should I try to make it sequential, or should each chapter be self sufficient? It naturally seems to lend itself to the latter.

It cannot really be sequential, and neither are your current times.

Introduction

The change of humanity from separation to Oneness, from illusion to clarity, from war to peace, has been written about and predicted for hundreds of years. It is no longer in the distant future. It is upon us now. And as with any major change, it involves destruction as well as construction. The old has to be destroyed to make way for the new. This usually involves a time of conflict between the old and the new, before there is some settling to allow evolution of the new.

We are now living through that time of conflict. Old establishments, institutions and systems are tumbling down as they must. Misdeeds are coming to light in order to hasten that process. Fear abounds as many feel the rugs being pulled from under their feet, with only uncertainty in sight to rely on. At the same time there is a surge of insight, courage and innovation, pushing upward like a lotus through the dry encrusted earth.

The environment is mirroring that change and confusion with quakes, tornados, fires, volcanos and bizarre weather. People feel swirled about and disoriented by the changes that seem to be happening so fast and in such unprecedented ways. How to survive and navigate these extreme times, when polarities seem stretched to their utmost? The purpose of this book is to offer something reliable to hold onto, a compass in the storm. The chapters may be viewed independently, depending on your need at the time. As you journey through these times you may find solace and insight by re-reading chapters you did not relate to before.

May this book serve you well, so you not only weather the storm, but come through it into clear skies dancing.

Paula Hart

CHAPTER 1

Altering destiny

Many of you have started to wonder whether it is possible to reverse the effect of the slippery slide upon which you collectively find yourselves. 'Is the momentum not too great, and are the channels not too deep?' you ask yourselves. These are indeed trying questions. In guessing the answers to be in the affirmative, much motivation and courage may be lost. We are here to tell you that the answer is an encouraging one. It is indeed always possible to reverse destiny. It all depends upon your will.

There are times when the human race appears to have lost its ground, to be sinking in the quagmire of its own illusions. These are the times when there is the greatest potential for change. This is one of these times. Thus is there cause for celebration, not despair; for hope not hopelessness. This is the time for the potential making of the human race – for your collective homecoming. It is the time of the great awakening, and the dissolution of the collective blindfold. It is the time for you all to see again who you are, where you have come from and where you belong.

Were we to wind time backwards, we would soon

see the beginnings of man's fall into blindness. It was due to despair that he donned the blindfolds – so he would not have to see what he did not understand. It seemed safer to limit the spheres of vision to what could be readily interpreted and controlled. Thus did man gain a certain sense of security in his uncertain world. However these blindfolds, originally his apparent saviour, now hold the keys to his downfall.

It is time they were released.

In order to know how to release them, we need to see how they were formed in the first place. So let us journey back… to a time when all was still and the world hardly formed as you now know it.

In the beginning

Imagine blackness, with scatterings of light; fuming vapours and starry explosions; voids and creations; showers of sparks and great comets of brightness overcoming each other in infinite space. Gradually your earth was formed, took shape and purpose, and began turning as it still does. Mountains rose and oceans settled; rivers bubbled up and rushed down to the sea; stars formed constellations in the night sky; and in the day the hot sun nurtured new vegetation. Slowly, slowly, life differentiated on your planet – swimming, digging, crawling, flying and finally walking. The colours of creation overtook each other in an effort to impress, on land, in sea and sky. The textures, flavours, scents and sounds multiplied endlessly to form the most exquisite concert of experiences for earth's residents.

Man stretched, yawned and looked around. 'Not a bad place' he thought. 'I'll make this mine.' And this is where he made his first error. He did not know he could not own the earth – not even a small bit of it. For it owns itself. But he tried, and we give him credit for the fact that he worked at it for thousands of years! He tried by dominating the other creatures, by regulating the vegetation and by 'sharing' earth with other humans. Different groups each claimed a patch that was called theirs – their country, their home.

He took whatever was in his 'patch' to be his property, and helped himself to anything he could use from it. He learned he could trade with others for what his 'patch' didn't offer.

All this kept him very busy. Too busy to notice that his whole raison d'etre was based on a misassumption: he could not own the earth or anything upon it. It owns itself.

When one tries to take something which is already owned, problems arise. And this is what happened. Instead of identifying as part of the earth, man pitted himself against her, thus alienating himself from his life source.

Donning the Blindfold

The pain of this isolation had to be ameliorated somehow, so greed, distraction and competition came into play. Soon man was as much against man as against the earth. However, even though the whole system was not working, man could not see another way, so deeply entrenched was he. The occasional truth-bearer was so threatening to the existing order, that in many cases he was sacrificed for the sake of the status quo. With each of these sacrifices, man donned a thicker blindfold. Puzzled and lost, feeling like powerless specks in a huge universe, man retreated into materialism, power plays and mindless diversions. Anything to keep the inner reality at bay.

Meanwhile, a force was growing elsewhere. This was a force of light and hope; of love and truth; of compassion and concern. This force, made of many beings in other realms and dimensions, witnessed the despair of both man and the earth, and resolved to help. Gradually these beings drew light into the souls of many men, until there were so many truth-bearers that others started to listen. Perhaps there were some alternative ways, after all.

Heading for home

At this point, man is on his way home. He is heading for a reunion with himself and all that is truly dear to him. And he will leave behind all that has led him away from his heart and his reality. However, man is made up of many individuals, all at different stages of evolution. There are still those deeply lost in the morass of power play, domination and materialism, who will not want the play to end. So, naturally, there will be turmoil, as there is at any ending and before any significant new beginning. This turmoil will be felt on a grand scale and also on an individual level, by each individual who becomes aware of his blindfold and the need to shed it. Change is never easy, but this one will be the most worthwhile you could collectively make. It will lead you to the paradise which you had thought could only be a myth.

There has never been a time on your planet when all was still, or going according to a plan. For all is always in motion and man's will plays a part in this. Changes are best not judged as good or bad – they are merely part of the pattern of the evolution of your world. Thus it is with the current situation. However, you are now heading towards a giant evolutionary step. The wheels are already in motion, and there is no turning back. Our aims in this book are to help you make this transition as smoothly as possible. In so doing you will be benefiting yourselves, and many others.

Surrendering to change

While your changes are in progress, you will be asking many questions of yourselves and others. 'What is going on? Where is this leading? How can I adapt so much, so fast?' We suggest you do not spend much time on seeking the answers. There may be no answers. The important thing is to surrender to the process of change, not necessarily to understand it fully. For while you are adapting and adjusting to these huge shifts you may be disorientated and not always thinking clearly. Therefore, even more than usual, your thinking will be less trustworthy than your feeling. Here we do not refer to emotions, but to your heart, your intuition, which has a hotline to the truth. So give your heads a rest and follow your hearts when in the midst of the greatest changes. These are the changes which may cause you to doubt your own judgement, which may have you wondering if you are going crazy! This will only be because you will be responding to parts of yourself you have not responded to before. There will be parts of you opening up, becoming accessible and wanting to be heard. In responding to these newly opened dimensions of yourself, you will be strengthening them and expanding yourself. So no matter how much your decisions surprise you, if they feel right, follow them. Let your head be the follower, not the leader. These will be times when intuition is crucial, and the decisions based on it will be the right ones, which will lead to the evolution of your planet and all on her.

It may come as no surprise to you now that the world order is shifting in this radical way. You have known it is not sustainable for long enough. So celebrate! You are alive at the most momentous time of human history, and it is not by accident, but by your own design, that this is so. You have all chosen to be here.

You have chosen to be here – every one of you. Why? Because you knew you would have an important role to play in this great unfolding drama. Each one of you will make a unique contribution to its course. And the course it takes will make a unique difference to each of you. So you are all here in an interdependent capacity.

For each of you the future will unfold uniquely, based on your soul's aims in being here at this time. It will also depend upon how much you use your free will to follow your soul.

Roles in the drama

Most of you reading this book will have chosen to be here to foster a peaceful transition. Others will have chosen to be here to help create change by destroying the current order. Yet others will have come to capitalise on the ensuing chaos. Even these last ones have a higher purpose. Theirs is to eventually realise the error of their current ways and to see the benefits of another choice. When one of these mistaken ones awakens, there is a great shift which affects all on Earth. Thus they too play their part in your collective evolution. So do not undervalue anyone on your current stage, or waste any time on blaming and looking for culprits. All will be playing their allotted roles as planned. And all will benefit in their own ways.

It may seem a slow process at times, when you are itching for a new world of fairness and beauty. But it must take the time it needs. Each step of the process is a valid part upon which the next step will be built. There are no short-cuts in such a process.

Stages of change

Change must be followed by adaptation and consolidation. It cannot be followed instantly by more change, or too much instability will occur. You all know this, so this is how you will be structuring the ensuing years. When the great changes happen, you will breathe faster and claim it is too much to adjust to, but you will manage. And after each event there will be a time of quietness – the relative calm before the next storm. Use these times of relative calm to gather yourself and your resources; to stabilise and consolidate. During these times you will find you may have extra energy and inspiration. This is because you will have shifted to a place of higher frequency, and many of the lower frequencies which were sapping your energy will have dropped off you. It will literally be like shedding an old skin. You may be tempted to accomplish great things at these times of lightness and inspiration. If this is the case, be careful not to burn yourself out. You will need to drink plenty of water, and rest often, to accommodate the changes well. Remember, your body is still a machine, and changes in frequency may affect it in various ways.

There are those who claim that great urgency is at hand. That if you do not all wake up quickly, you are all doomed. This is not how it is. Let us explain how we see it:

Picture the sun rising and shining upon a closed flower. The flower gradually opens, eventually revealing its great beauty and shining back at the sun. At sunset, it starts to close its petals again, and when the moon is high, the flower has become the bud it was before. It has returned to mere potential.

Now if that flower had not managed to open fully by sunset, its potential would still be there. It would just not yet have actualised its potential. Thus it is with man. The potential will always be there. It cannot die. The question is only whether man will actualise his potential before sunset. In your case sunset refers to the end of the Earth's capacity to continue as a viable host. The flower may have little influence over the sun, but man has great influence over the Earth and her ability to continue as host. So each of you has two important tasks: to care for and help detoxify the Earth, and to self-actualise or awaken.

Man's interdependence with Earth

How you choose to perform these tasks will be different for each of you. If you listen to your souls, you will know what your own contribution is to be. You may have times of great uncertainty, in which you have no idea of your direction or even your power. But if your intent is strong, your listening quiet, and your discernment sharp, you will find your way. Before long, you will be told one way or another what you are to do, in your quest for a safer and saner world. It will not always be easy to listen and accept what you are told. This may entail yet more change. It may require courage, determination and perseverance. Developing these qualities will be part of your journey of self-actualisation. So it will all dovetail, and you will find yourself becoming a person you did not know you were. In fact you will be becoming more and more who you really are. And the more this happens, the more automatically you will care appropriately for the Earth. This is how interdependent this whole process is!

Responding to others

As you become more of who you are, you might find that others question you, as they may not be on the same journey as yours, or at the same stage. The trick in dealing with this will be to let them question you all they like. Just continue on your journey regardless. See their questions as just that: questions, not statements. Their questions merely indicate they do not understand. They indicate nothing about you or what you are doing, so do not take them personally, or you might trip up on them and waste valuable time. Sometimes they will put out questions disguised as statements, possibly as judgements. Again, see the question underlying these words, and answer or ignore it as you see fit. Do not feel responsible for these disguised questions. They do not belong to you. Your compassion may decree that you answer these pleas for enlightenment. That is fine, but remember you are not responsible for how your answer is received. That is the responsibility of the receiver. So do not enter into justification and lengthy reviews of your actions. Give your answer, if you must, and then let it go, and get on with your own travels. It is really each person for himself in this journey you are all embarked upon. You cannot self-actualise anyone but yourself!

During these times you may find you become much more open to criticism, more vulnerable and ready to see your own mistakes and past path more clearly. This is a good sign, and indicates you are becoming more aware, and therefore more open to new choices. It is only when you are ready to leave behind old patterns that you will embrace new ones. While this will happen to the whole of humanity on a grand scale, it will be happening to each of you as well. It is the old story of the macrocosm and the microcosm once again. So when you feel remorse, guilt or disillusionment about your past actions, accept that these feelings are a part of that process. Accept these feelings, then let them go and move on into the present. Let yourself go with the flow of your own evolution without putting any barriers in the way.

RIDING THE CHANGE

CHAPTER 2

The end of time...

Humans have fought, struggled and conquered, over millennia. It has been a pattern which has prevailed, out of need- the need for experience, for survival, for comfort and safety. But soon, these ways will no longer be needed.

The human race is about to enter paradise, literally. We tell you this so that you can prepare yourselves, as you would for any new destination.

This destination is beyond your imaginings. It is made of beauty and truth, and will not hold anything other than these. There will be a resonance which will not sustain anything in conflict with love. Therefore, the sooner you know how to connect with love, the sooner you can access this paradise.

'Where do I buy the ticket?' you are asking. You buy it within yourself. 'What does it cost?' Everything. 'How do I get one?' Through asking for one. We will spend a little time elucidating these answers, as these few words may not entirely satisfy your curiosity!

Heading to paradise

The ticket to paradise is easily obtained, because,

ultimately, the tram on which you are all travelling will be stopping there. It is a case of which stops may hold you up on the way, and whether you will get off the tram before it arrives at paradise. There will be many stops along the way. Humankind is choosing the nature of these stops right now. Some people are choosing to get off the tram earlier, offering their places to others, or helping others in the future from higher realms. Some are being the conductors on the tram, ensuring everyone has a seat and no-one sticks chewing gum on the windows! Some are driving the tram – not always on the most efficient route. Many are busy reading or knitting, barely stopping to look at the view outside. Some are dreaming of what the destination might be like; others are dreaming of what they hope it won't be like.

The destination is written in the little window at the front of the tram. PARADISE. This much is set. But the route is a magical one, dictated by the minds of the passengers. This is a tram which can switch tracks any time – it can even create new tracks as it goes along. Be not fooled by appearances. There is not one view which all the passengers see out of the window. Every passenger creates her own view on this tram. And every passenger creates her own tram stops, although some are created by so many people that they appear to be shared by all.

The journey to wisdom

To reach paradise, a human must have alighted at a sufficient number of stops, and therefore have a great number of experiences. Through these experiences, the well-travelled human will have started upon the path towards wisdom.

To get your ticket for the best route, choose experiences which will foster your wisdom.

There is much misunderstanding about wisdom. It is not a cognitive concept, or an amassing of knowledge. It is a connection with knowing, which comes about as a result of seeking, of experiencing, and of being open to clearly perceiving. It does not necessarily come with age, and it certainly does not correlate with status or wealth. Wisdom is a gentle art – made of looking, listening and inwardly digesting. It is made of discernment and of introspection. It comes from a silence and receptivity. Judgement is the enemy of wisdom, as it shuts the doors of perception.

So seek your wisdom in quietness, in solitude and in openness. It always comes to those who ask, as does everything which the soul seeks.

Upside down reality

Before long, you will find, once you have asked, that you start having insights which surprise you. They may not fit with what you think you know – they might threaten to unseat you completely. This is because the tram driver you have collectively chosen has taken you on some rather strange and devious routes, which have taken you further from wisdom, rather than closer to it. So the view you are used to seeing out the window may be very foreign to wisdom. This means that when you see wisdom for the first time, you may well believe it to be utter nonsense, as it bears so little relationship to your known 'reality'.

Do not be fooled into believing illusion is the truth. This is the time for the truth to be revealed in your world, and it is the first time humankind is ready to receive it consciously.

We told you the cost of the ticket to paradise was 'everything'. Perhaps you can begin to understand that, if wisdom means embracing a different reality, it also means discarding the current one.

The old and the new

This means that many of your systems of structure and belief may need to be challenged, and either changed or discarded. So there will be many protests of one form or another – some peaceful, some not so peaceful. This is an inevitable part of your collective ride now. 'Realities' do not leave easily. It is a struggle to change from one reality to another. At times it may feel like tearing off your own skin. But it is only a shedding of illusion, and of habits. Habits die hard, but die they must. Blindfolds do not assist clear vision. This process of change will inevitably cause conflict among you, as there are those who already see reality, and those who fight to uphold the old illusions. There will be much fighting between the old and the young, many of whom have come into this lifetime in a state of well-developed wisdom.

During these times of change, you would be well-advised to stay indoors, out of trouble, keeping your head low. Is this what you are saying to yourselves? This response to the situation is indeed an unhelpful one. If the aim is the wisdom of the human race, keeping out of sight and safely tucked away will not add to that process. No, indeed, this is the time to speak out, to those who will hear. It is the time to muster whatever wisdom you already have, and share it with those who seek it. Let it breed in fertile grounds, for there are many of those. Do not seek direct conflict, by pushing reality at those still tied to their illusions, but subtly leave it where they may find it when ready. For at some point, they, too, will want it.

Butterflies of time

So, dear ones, you are on the most exciting journey: from delusion to clarity; from paralysis to power; from Earth to paradise. You are indeed the butterflies of your time, about to emerge from the chrysalis into spectacular glory.

Eden was a version of what you will encounter. Beauty was there, and truth, but it was at a denser vibration than the paradise you are headed for. Your paradise is very light, and vibrates at a high frequency. Many of you would not yet be compatible with this frequency, and therefore would be unable to access it. So, one of your tasks now is to raise the frequency of your vibrations. There are many ways you can do this. It takes practise, as does any skill, so have patience and perseverance.

Matching paradise

Firstly, remember, you have an electro-magnetic field. This field affects who you are – your thoughts, feelings, intuition, ambitions; and how you are –

your mental, emotional, spiritual, interpersonal and physical health. It affects your development, in every way. True wisdom is dependent upon connection with a large range of frequencies. This enables the wise person to access understanding from a variety of sources at a higher vibratory level. Most of you don't have trouble accessing lower frequencies, as that is an evolutionary stage you have mastered. However, few of you know how to actively facilitate a higher vibratory rate. Here is an exercise for you to try. Keep breathing throughout!

Star jump exercise:

*See yourself under the stars again ....
imagine yourself to be upon a bright shining one
.... out there in the starry
universal sky ....
from your own bright star, gaze out ..... at the deep
midnight blue space, studded with diamond stars
.... an endless blanket of twinkling lights
.... now choose a star in the far distance
.... and leap across space to
it .... you are upon it and
within its brightness ....
.... now leap to
a further one ....
and a further one.............................. and
again .... to one even further away ....
and once more, take that leap to a distant star
....now stop
there and feel what it is like to be on that star
....*

*feel the quality of its brightness around and
through you .... how does
your body feel while you are there ....
.... do you feel
lighter... heavier ...... any unusual sensations
.... stay there for a while, noticing how
your body feels .... keep breathing ....
....
....
....
.... now slowly return to the chair, bed or floor
you are on .... become aware of your surroundings
.... notice the changes in your
body ....
....*

*When you feel solidly grounded and back in the room
again, open your eyes.*

You have just visited a higher frequency. You may
have noticed various sensations as you moved further
out of your usual range. They are the gauge, for you to
know something is happening. This is an exercise you
can train yourself with, just as you would train for a
sport. Try aiming for stars that are further away each
time, ensuring all of you goes with you on your leap.

There are many ways to accomplish the same thing.
This one is quick, easy and endless in its potential.

Love is the pivot

We would speak to you now of love, yet again. It is
not a state which you can conjure up, unless you are at
the right vibratory rate. It is impossible to experience

love, when you are in a state of low vibration. Love does not resonate with a low vibration. Desire and other emotions and drives do, but not love. Paradise is built out of love. Many of your illusions about love are waiting to be shattered, so that it may emerge in its true beauty.

We keep coming back to the issue of love, as do all your major religions. This is because it is the pivot around which your world turns. This is why so much has been said about love over the millennia. However, when concepts are put into words, they inevitably lose much of their integrity. Words always have a context, whereas concepts like love do not. In trapping them into a context, you kill a part of their essence. All you can do is try to describe them – you can never really capture them in words. So the more love has been talked about in your world, the more that talk has strayed from the truth. The truth of love is actually incredibly simple. It is the energy which holds everything together; it is unlimited; it is effervescent; it is available to all. That's about it.

Accessing love

When you are resonating with the love vibration your thoughts and actions will be influenced by it. But you cannot capture more love through behaving one way or another. The only way to go about capturing it is to resonate with it. As this is your natural state, this means that if you lower your barriers and be who you are, you will be in love. You natural state is one of goodness and light. So there is some correlation between goodness and love, but not in the way most of your religions express put it. It is not a case of 'be good now' and then you will get to heaven later. You will get to heaven eventually, no matter what you do now. But it is how you get there which you can determine. If you allow your true nature to emerge and resonate with the love vibration, you will be healthier and happier on the journey; and it will be a more direct route.

CHAPTER 3

Time to move

You are all at the same stage, in a way, even though in some ways this may not seem so. What you all have in common is that you are perched at the cliff's edge. The differences between you will be reflected in the ways you deal with this position.

Some will try to save others from falling, some will push others over the edge in their attempts to return to safer, more familiar ground and others will take the leap and learn to fly. A few might even try to dynamite the cliff itself. For all of you, in one way or another, it is time to move.

For some this move may not take the form of an external shift, but only of an internal one – a shift of consciousness. For others the internal shift will be mirrored by an external one, and there will be much actual moving around of people to different destinations. Let this not perturb you as it happens in your immediate circle. It is a sign that the world of people is waking up at last, and should be viewed with celebration, not trepidation.

Breaking static energy patterns

Why will so many people need to physically move?

There are many reasons for this. One is that the static energy patterns formed by man need to be shifted by man's own movement, in order to be broken up and allow new patterns to emerge energetically. Nothing new can manifest on the physical plain, until it has manifest on the level of energy or consciousness. The moves required of many of you will instigate much consciousness change as well as physical change. There will be a shaking up of your kaleidoscope on all levels to enable new patterns to be formed on all levels. This is what man and the Earth now need, so this is what humanity is designing for itself.

Now you may find yourself in the midst of some turmoil: "But I don't want to change. I am happy just as I am." And this may be the case, that you are indeed fine just as you are. In fact it is undoubtedly the case, for each one of you. However, it is still the time to move. The tram is arriving at your stop and your soul will ensure you board it.

Resistance is futile

Resisting the changes that come your way will eventually prove futile. The more they are resisted the thicker and faster they will hit you, until you give in to them and go with their flow. This is no threat or punishment, it is purely a reflection of your own soul's determination that you should not miss the tram. It may also happen that while you bravely step aboard the tram you see others running the other way. These may even be your loved ones and close acquaintances. You may feel torn: "Do I hop off the tram and go with them, leave them behind, or try to pull them with me?" The answer to this will always be the same, hard though it may seem. Leave them behind. They will only be ready for a later tram, whereas you are ready for this one. This is one journey you must honour as yours alone. If you allow them to pull you back you are only creating a detour for both of you. By all means invite them to come with you, but if their answer is no, go anyway. It is your journey, not theirs. We are speaking here about movements of consciousness as well as of body.

The service of refugees

This need for the movement of many is one of the reasons you have created so many refugees. They are doing you all a service, although few of them realise it or enjoy it. They are helping to break up the crystalline structures you have formed over aeons of time, so they can reform into patterns which will better suit your future.

The movement will not always be on such a grand scale, however. Most of you can expect to be confronted with greater and more sudden changes than you were used to. These will stretch your consciousness beyond limits you held dear in the past, and enable you to embrace new frontiers of understanding.

Farewelling the known

There will be times when you doubt the direction in which you may be headed, as it may seem so unreal and different from your known way of life. At these times be sure to look into your heart, not your head, for guidance. Familiarity is not always a good yardstick. It may just be showing you the old crystalline structure which must be shattered before the new can be formed. This is when the leap off the cliff edge is required. Trust your process and go with it, no matter what you think it might bring. These are times of great surprises. If you follow your process well, it may bring something quite different from what you expect. The reason for this is that by following the process you are creating a new crystalline structure, out of which all sorts of hitherto unknown things may emerge. So while your expectations are based upon your past experience, the results of your process will not be. They will be based upon something quite new.

All this may sound quite confusing, and may have you shaking your heads. But later, as these changes occur, these words may take on new meaning for you. So we suggest you return to this book from time to time. As times change, you will get quite different insights from these chapters on re-reading them.

CHAPTER 4

Moving ahead with style

Style and grace are related. To develop your own style in the coming times will be imperative. To open yourself to receive divine grace will be even more so. Divine grace is a term we would like you to be acquainted with, as this, in a sense, may be your life-line later. We have already spoken of the need to look to yourself for guidance, but divine grace takes you a step further.

When miracles happen

While you wander along your path, sniffing the roses, there is another parallel path above you – the divine equivalent of your path. Every time your path coincides with this other path, we call that divine grace. At these times, extraordinary things happen, things that you cannot necessarily explain, but you know to be true. These occurrences give you a glimpse into another world, and also tie you into wider possibilities and opportunities than could otherwise have been the case. Divine grace can only happen at the meeting point of the two paths. It is like your tram coming to a junction, which gives the opportunity to change tracks and choose a new direction. These times in your life are the magical times, when the impossible happens with ease. They are sent to stretch your horizons and to give you shortcuts to your destiny.

Accessing the miraculous

We would like to discuss the ways in which you can best access these junction points.

Firstly, never doubt that you are observed all the time. As we have stated, you are never alone. The helpers you have allowed and chosen for your route through life are always there, subtly giving you pointers and offering you experiences to help you on your way. They are a bit like the parking attendants at a big sports event, waving the cars towards parking spots. It is ultimately your decision whether or not you follow their gesticulations. It usually saves time if you do, because they have more knowledge of the grounds than you do. You can of course decide to be independent and go down that other track to where you think there might be a closer spot, but you may well get there and find there is no spot at all, or the road is blocked off.

So, there they are, the guides, angels, and others, all collaborating to help you on your way. Your choices are: to believe they don't exist, to ignore their messages, to consider what they are showing you, or to blindly follow what you think they are indicating.

Following the clues

These are always your choices. We already hear you asking 'But how do we hear them – how do we know what they are telling us?' There are so many ways. There are inward ways and outward ways. The inward way is to be still, to listen within to the quiet voice that speaks to you in silence. Other inward ways are to listen to your dreams and themes. The directions of your waking and sleeping dream journeys can give you much food for thought. Clues which come to you in dreams will often turn into nightmares if not heeded. Waking themes may become obsessions if not listened to and acted upon. The sorts of themes we mean are ones such as loneliness, greed and other habitual ones, which seem to stalk you wherever you go. If they come into your awareness as issues, you are being offered the opportunity to change them. The themes are there to be heard, to be responded to in some constructive way, leading to change and growth. Each time you respond to these message in this way, you are bringing your path closer to the higher parallel one.

Synchronicity

Outward ways of receiving messages from your helpers are many. You have by now probably heard much about synchronicity – those events where time seems to have collided your inner events with your outer ones. The number plate on the car in front tells you the answer to the problem you have been mulling over; the woman in front of you in the bank queue tells her friend about a similar situation to yours, from a different viewpoint; you switch on the radio only to hear someone reiterating exactly what you have just learned. There are other ways too, in which your choices are put clearly before you. You are shown mirrors of your traits in other people, in order to become familiar with your ways and your choices. Situations confront you in which you have to make a choice, and this choice then gives you cause to reflect. The ways in which your helpers arrange things for your edification is endless. The point is for you to learn. And learn you do.

Cul-de-sacs and grace

The problem is that sometimes you take on board learnings which are not helpful – ones which lead to dead-ends in terms of your growth. To help you undo these false learnings, the helpful beings have to work extra hard.

However, every now and then you may strike a time when you are completely ready for a lesson you really do need to learn. When this is the case, amazing things can happen. Firstly, the event appears which gives you the lesson. Then, if you have taken it on board, you are in a new space, in a way. Into that space can come new experiences – ones which, in your outgrown mode, would not have been possible. That is when 'miracles' happen. They are fostered by attitudes of newness, of openness and of readiness. These 'miracles' are manifestations of divine grace. They are the universe saying 'You have come up to meet us, so we can now show you something new.' This newness may take the form of an apparently impossible occurrence; a sudden way out of an apparently impossible dilemma; or a gift. These are events which the human being, no matter how hard he tries, cannot accomplish alone.

Divine intervention is necessary. In fact, sometimes the harder the human being tries to accomplish them, the further he pushes them out of reach. The strength of his will leaves no space for anything else to enter and help him. Sometimes, when this individual finally gives up, is when he gets his prize, simply because he has, at last, made space.

Making space

We are telling you all this because in the days and weeks to come, you may find that you cannot accomplish all you want to by yourself. There may be difficult times, or times when you want to achieve more than seems possible. It is at these times that you may receive the most help, if you make space for it. There may come times when your insight precedes your change – when you are therefore impatient with yourself. Divine grace is unlikely to enter into a room of impatience. So keep noticing, and aiming, without judging. This is the most welcoming room for divine grace. Emotions and thoughts can form a rut in your system, into which you can slip. When you are down there it is hard for new information to reach you. This is one of the reasons we have suggested you remain slightly above and beyond difficult times, and detach yourself from negative or ruminative emotions quickly. If you are able to do that, you are not too full for divine grace to enter and change things for you.

CHAPTER 5

Unfurling the flag

Where you have been and where you are going are two different places, in a sense. And in another sense they are just the same. You will roll up the flag of the identity of your country, and unfurl a new one, while standing in the same spot. You are not going to be taken to some foreign land, which is named Paradise. Instead you are going to discover that paradise is already where you are. When your blindfolds are lifted, you will see it for the first time. This may be quite a shock – to discover that the reality you thought you knew was only a cover. But luckily, when your blindfolds are gone, this will not perturb you nor interest you. You will be fully where and when you are.

New laws and pure being

It might as well be a different country, for it will follow different laws – or rather, its occupants will. The laws of Karma, and cause and effect will be gone. Their purpose was for evolvement, learning and range of experience. These will no longer be your aims. By the time you access paradise, these aims will have been fulfilled. Instead your aim in paradise will be pure existence. This means your aim will be to be. It is no more complex than this. You will still have free will, which will dictate how you choose to be, but your soul will no longer have an agenda for you to follow. You will have completed the agenda. Instead of guiding you subtly despite your unconsciousness, you soul will now have free rein to express itself in full consciousness in your every moment. It will no longer be your soul versus your personality. They will be as one. This will lead to great peace – the so-called 'peace that passes all understanding.' There will therefore be virtually no inner conflict, which means there will be virtually no outer conflict, between people, animals and the environment. All will be in a state of harmony. Because of this, much bliss will be felt.

Please understand this: paradise is not a place. It is a state of being, of consciousness.

It is the state you are working towards, or preferably playing towards, right now, in reading this book.

Paradise and the death of conflict

Much has been written about this elusive paradise of yours. And many of the writings were fictitious, based on the illusions and fantasies of unconscious writers only too eager to externalise paradise into a place you could access with a bit of luck. While the mindset of the human collective remains the same, no place is paradise, and every place is frought with conflict. In a way you will create paradise yourselves, although in another way, it is already there, in place, waiting to be accessed in each of you. You may catch glimpses of it now and then, when you are at peace, or in nature, but they will only be short-lived as the human collective has much power to lower frequencies. To retain your own paradise despite this pull is rare indeed. However, it will become easier and easier, as humanity changes, density is shed and the collective frequency rises. Then there will come a timeless time when you all forget what this world was like before – when conflict and pain no longer even exist in the human memory. There will only be variations of bliss.

The roadless road to bliss

Everything you are experiencing in your world now is part of the road to this bliss. There is not one act, thought or word that is not forming the paving of this road. It may seem at times as though there are retrograde steps happening; as though there is no hope for humanity and your world. But do not believe this is so. You cannot always see how the pieces fit together. We have a better view, and can see the perfection in every detail. The destination is there and will be reached. We are just trying to help you avoid the potholes in the road. You still have suffering as part of your world, and we would help you to avoid this needlessly.

There are so many watching your progress with concern and love. We know you will get there, and are wanting you to get there as painlessly as possible, and with the Earth as intact as possible. The Earth is very special and may still be there in this form into timelessness. She has other forms too, which you cannot yet access, but which will become apparent as your frequencies rise. You will be able to choose which of these forms you inhabit or visit, once you have developed enough to access them all. This will be a source of great joy, as they will all be beautiful, in different ways.

Be yourself

Do not worry about how and when you will 'get there.' There is no way for you to plan this. It is not as if following any particular technique will lead you to paradise. You each need to go through whatever steps you need to go through. It is an individual process. There is absolutely no recipe, whatever anyone might tell you. So follow your own process as it arises. Just take the next step. That is all you can do. And one day you will wake up and find you are there. You will then realise the irrelevance of anyone else's progress to yours. The only important thing will be to be yourself.

CHAPTER 6

Loosening the ties

Saying goodbye is never easy – not when you love what you are leaving. Expect to learn to say goodbye soon, if you have not already. In journeying along your road you will need to depart from, as much as you will need to approach. The hellos and the goodbyes may be in balance, but the goodbyes may seem harder to you. You will need to learn the art of detachment.

In following your own road, you may need to leave behind possessions, places, people, habits, and aspects of what you have come to regard as yourself. Parting from some of them may almost require surgery. But if the time comes for parting, and that parting does not happen, you will find yourself on a detour instead of your main road.

You will need to learn to loosen the ties between yourself and all the externals. This involves awareness that you are not these externals, nor do you need to depend upon them. For many of you, these insights are not easily accepted. You have been successfully brainwashed by those who would enslave you all. Many of you believe you are your clothes, your job, your children, your house, your personality. Therefore it is natural that the thought of parting with any of these instils a deep panic and a holding on with the fingernails to prevent loss. The good news we would remind you of again, is that none of these is the real you. So should you lose any or all of them, you would remain completely intact. This may sound silly, and you may be saying 'of course, I know that!' But many of you, when it comes to the test, think and act as though you do not remember that.

Parting tips

Spending time just being who you are in silence, may help your sense of true identity, and thus your ability to detach from what is not you. When the time comes to part with what was once useful for you, be it a relationship, a habit, a house or whatever, you will find it easier to part once you have acknowledged what that item, quality or person meant to you, and what it gave you. Thank it for its contribution, then you will be freer to move on. This way you will have completed the interaction properly, with no untied ends to call you back. Then let it go and look firmly into the present, without looking back. The occasional happy memory is harmless enough, but they may be addictive, causing you to lose the present in your visitations of the past. Wonderful present opportunities may thus slip by unnoticed, which seems a waste, as the past offers no opportunities other than temporary escape.

Detachment as freedom

Detachment does not make you less available. On the contrary, it enables you to be fully available, as you are not being partially owned by external things and people. Some of you equate detachment with aloofness, with being detached from the present – somehow off in a little cloud, away from everyone else. This is not what we are talking about here. Detachment is a knowing that you, as a being, are independent of all external props, and thus can view their loss with equanimity. This leads to the knowledge of your true power. Equate detachment with freedom, and you will be halfway towards understanding it.

The power of hope

As well as detachment, in order to release yourself from your past, you will need hope. This is the ability to see beyond current difficulties and know that 'things will work out'. Hope will give you the strength you need to see awkward moments through, and to let go of the past, knowing the future will be supportive. So look for clues that give you hope. It is a valuable commodity.

CHAPTER 7

Completion

At the end of the day, you go home, settle into your favourite chair and relax. This is what humanity is about to do. We are telling you the same things in many different ways. Repetition is often needed before new information transforms into understanding.

After a time of turmoil, you will enter the time of completion. You will have explored, created, fought, struggled, played, felt, destroyed, competed, avoided, mastered and done countless other things. You will have done what you wanted to do within the framework of the separateness you invented for yourselves. Your day away from home will be over, and it will be time to come back to base.

Picture a rainy field with two teams of little boys playing soccer. They are expending much energy, running about very busily all trying to accomplish something, whether it is to score goals, to get the ball or avoid the ball! On the side-lines are the mothers, yelling encouragement from under dripping umbrellas. As the game progresses, the wet field gets more churned up and slippery; and the players get muddier. Many are relieved when at last the final whistle is blown and each mother can gather a soggy son and retreat into the comfort of a warm car. At home there are hot showers and mugs of steaming soup. Muddy wet boots and socks are replaced with warm dry socks. After all the cold and exertion, it is a welcome respite.

Paths to the warmth of home

Humanity has almost finished its great game of soccer. It is almost time for the warmth of home again. But first there is the churned up, slippery field to contend with a while longer. The young soccer players know they have a choice. They can play safe, go slow and risk scoring no goals, in order to avoid getting muddier. They can go hell-for-leather into the fray, with no regard for mud or sliding, and will probably slip and fall. Or they can take the middle path of boldness with caution, going for it where it looks less slippery, and slowing down in the wet patches. This way they will probably avoid injury, and may still score some goals. Observation and discrimination are required to successfully manage the bold cautious way.

Your choices in the coming times will be similar. You may try to hide from the 'mud' of the world, but in so doing will be shielding yourself from opportunities which could lead to your growth and your path home. You may rush headlong into battle with the forces you seek to oppose, creating for yourself needless heartache or worse. Or you may look, listen and then proceed with care and courage. This will be the safest and most effective way in your coming times. If you follow this recipe, you will not be depriving yourself of opportunity or of choice.

CHAPTER 8

Totality

Until you have understood the patterns behind the workings of your world, there will be unrest and a lack of peace. For you to begin to understand these patterns, there must be a break in your routine. This is the only way to distract you from your everyday concerns.

Eye-opening world events

So there will be more and more events which will trigger an understanding that you are all linked. You will be seeing more clearly how your welfare is interdependent. You will be shown how, if one group suffers, the rest of you suffer too. These will need to be events on a world scale, to open your eyes to world-scale connections. Big questions will be raised in your minds, which normally you would be too 'busy' to think about. The meaning of things, of choices and of occurrences, will loom large at last. You will have cause to pause, again and again, until you see what it is all about. Environmental issues will raise their heads repeatedly too, until you understand that the Earth, air, water and space are interdependent parts of the oneness of your lives. The environment you all depend upon may have to show you just how dependent you are, before you wake up to this fully.

The more you understand, the less these reminders will be needed. The whole creates only what it needs. When you understand your interconnectedness fully, there will be peace, completely.

The single web of life

Begin now to see your whole existence and universe as one huge functioning web of life, for this is what it is. Each of you is one small but unique part. There is no part that is separate from any other part, nor is there any part which can exist without all the others. The notion of separateness is complete fiction. It was only an idea that sprang up in the fertile mind of man. No other part of this great web entertains such an idea. Every other part knows of its connectedness, and humbly plays its role as the puzzle-piece without which there would be no complete picture. It is only man who dares to declare himself above the laws of nature. For man and nature, this cannot and will not happen much longer. Soon you will all know your place in the greater scheme of things. And what a relief that will be for all concerned!

The dance of life will continue to play itself out whatever man does or does not do: Man is by no means the pivot around which life turns. But he is collectively an important part, like all others, and is currently at a turning point. That is part of the dance. For man and the Earth, particularly, it is important that this turn is carefully and consciously negotiated. As man is part of the web, how he goes forward will affect all life. But most obviously of all, it will affect man himself.

The paradox of perfection

We know it is hard for you to understand paradox. In your world of logic there is room only for black and white. An object must be square or round – it cannot be both. But the truth of your world is full of paradox. This is because it contains everything. So everything in your world is perfect, exactly as it is. Yet there is much in your world which could bear changing. There is much sorrow, much grief and sense of incompletion, much hunger and misery. This is so, yet this is exactly how it is meant to be now. Within each of you there is perfection. You are exactly as you are meant to be right now. Yet, each of you has areas yet to evolve. Mankind seems to have created a near disaster in his care-taking of his planet and of his brothers; yet this is quite in order. There is now an urgency for change and recognition; yet there is no urgency at all, for all is already in a state of perfection. The human mind struggles to comprehend how this can all be so. Your mind must bend past all the education you have given it, to see the truth in the lack of logic. Gradually, with experience, this will come to you. You will understand that all is not as it seems at one level, then another and another. Eventually you will see that all is perfect in its imperfection, yet there is still room for evolvement, which only unfolds what is already there.

Creator and created are one

When this times comes, you will know that you are

indeed only a component. Yet you are also the creator of it all. For there is no separation between the creator and the created. It is all one energy, one power. This is why, although you alone seem small and insignificant at times, you are not. You have the power of creation behind you, and if you harness this in moving forward, you are a mighty force. This may give rise to another confusing paradox. While there is no separation and you all have equal power (you are power), due to free will you may not have access to your true power. If consciously you believe yourself to be but a powerless cog in the great wheel of destiny, turning regardless of your wishes, you will not be accessing much of your creative power. You will have given it away to the concept of helplessness.

Consciousness is power

If, on the other hand, you know yourself to be a part of the creative force of your universe, you are indeed that, and will be able to change much. So, the more understanding you have, the more of your power you can claim. Ultimately, for humanity, consciousness is power. So foster the growing of your consciousness in whatever ways you choose. Remember, as a part of the web, when your consciousness expands, it is not you alone who is affected. A great ripple goes out changing many lives, when you change.

CHAPTER 9

Communicating

Gently does it

The best way to get a message across is always with gentleness. The receiver of the message has no reason to close off and defend, if the message is gently given. Remember this in the coming times, when differences will prevail and there will be much ramming of opinions down throats! There may be the temptation to join in the general madness, shouting your truth for all to hear whether they like it or not. But it would be more effective to stand on the side-lines and be your truth. Let others see it demonstrated, rather than spoken of. Humanity has always learnt more from experience than from words, which are so often a distortion.

Rumours

In these times of movement and change, there will be many rumours circulating. There will be rumours of hope and rumours of disaster; of potential war and annihilation; of potential salvation and bliss. We suggest you listen to none of them at all. Find your own truth, for this will be the only one that applies to you.

All of these rumours will probably have some basis in truth, and may apply to some people. Your story will be your story alone. So rumours will serve no purpose except to confuse. There will be those who purposely seek to confuse or frighten, through creating and spreading rumours. You will be exercising your power by defusing and ignoring these messages. The future is never fixed in any case, so exactly what is predicted may never come to pass. The more people credit a rumour as the truth, the more that rumour is likely to manifest in the future. Belief creates reality.

Truth

There will always be many versions of truth. It is different for different people. Perceptions of truth depend upon the frequency at which the perceiver resonates. Those who resonate at similar frequencies will share similar truths. This does not mean any particular version of the truth is the right one. Humans have taken the word 'truth' and thrust upon it the responsibility of carrying a great many things. 'The truth' is seen to be the ultimate compass by which to steer one's course, if one is a 'good' person. 'The truth' is seen as the ultimate alibi – the excuse for all sorts of words and deeds. 'The truth' is seen as the epitome of innocence. In fact, the truth is none of these. These are all man's distortions and manipulations of it. There is only one ultimate truth, and that is 'I am'. It is the indisputable absolute.

So the 'truths' you are told by others, as well as the ones you espouse yourself, always bear a little scrutiny. 'Discrimination before blind belief' is a useful motto here.

CHAPTER 10

Limitless destiny

There are those of you who believe yourselves to be beyond the normal 'rat-race' of humanity; who have struggled and achieved a hard won peace and insight into yourselves and the human condition. To you we dedicate this chapter.

You are already a long way up the staircase and perhaps need some different guidance from that offered to the multitudes still struggling on the lower steps. This is not to denote any form of superiority or inferiority, merely the state of being and of readiness for information. If you are indeed one for whom this chapter is intended, you will already know this. Whereas if you are not, you might take offence at this differentiation. If so, please skip to the next chapter, for you are not ready for this one.

Walking your path

There are countless ways of reaching your destination, and you sometimes wonder at the choices you see spread out before you. They may seem baffling in the extreme, and as you are intent upon 'doing your best', you may get swept into some self-doubt about whether the roads you choose are the most suitable ones. We would like to discuss this from a few different angles, in order to help you gain clarity and avoid such confusion in the future.

Firstly, please know that whatever path you choose will always be the right one for you. For it is not the path, but the way you walk it, which determines where it takes you. The best path in the world may take you nowhere at all, if you do not walk it with courage and determination; and the path which appears a cul-de-sac at the outset, may be turned into a freeway by the set of your gait. So do not waste energy on questioning the choices you are following. Look only at how you are following them. You will create the opportunities you need and you will learn from them, provided your attitude is open. Whoever you meet on that path will then also benefit, not only by your example, but by the energy of your being, which will be in harmony with itself.

Otherworldly help

Secondly, know too that you are always protected, wherever you go. You have chosen, in a sense, an arduous and sometimes lonely path. This choice attracts the attention of many well-meaning beings in other realms, who appoint themselves then to help you in your chosen tasks. This is not because you are any more special or favoured than anyone else. It is because you are operating at a frequency which these beings can access. You are on their wave-length, if you like, so they can help you more easily. So let this knowledge give you added courage.

Stretching into new shapes

Thirdly, the lack of short-term happiness or ease in a situation does not mean there is something 'wrong' with what you or someone else has done. You and others will create 'glitches' in the path, in order to give you the opportunity of learning and stretching beyond your usual comfort zones. How else does one stretch than with some discomfort? Sure, the piece of elastic might rather sit in its short, static form on the shelf, but it has been designed to be put to use, and this involves some pulling and tugging and changing of shape. So bear the tugging and allow yourself to be formed by it into new shapes. Do not let past formations, habits and expectations mould you back into what once was. Rather look towards the limitlessness of your future, and let these apparently awkward or unhappy situations help you towards this. Remember, your future will bear little resemblance to your past. We mean this in every way – inner and outer.

Fools rush in ...

Fourth, remember to tie your shoelaces firmly before you run. This may sound like foolish advice to those who have already progressed so far, but there is more to it than you think! You may, at times, become very enthusiastic about a certain course of action – sure that this is the next right step for you. However, you may take off too soon, having disregarded a few salient points. Enthusiasm, integrity and energy are all very well, but they must be matched with perspicacity and wisdom if they are not to cause uproar on a regular basis. We will take you through some of the points, which you would be wise to consider before embarking on any important venture – be it a sentence, an action or a new direction.

1. Could you have misunderstood what you consider to be 'the facts'? This happens only too often, and is the cause of many additional misunderstandings. Particularly when you are operating from a place of higher frequency than many around you are, misunderstandings may easily occur, and to respond from the basis of one of them can lead to all sorts of unnecessary entanglements. So, particularly during heated moments, ask yourself to stop and reconsider your sureness of 'the facts'. Look at it from the other direction, and see if it looks the same, before you leap in. This may be easier for you than for the person who operates from a lower frequency, as you have probably been where he is, whereas he probably has not been where you are.

2. Before you rush headlong into action, consider whether you know enough about what you are doing. It may be that you see the validity of what you want to do, but others around you do not, and your words or action would cause unnecessary conflict. In these cases, sometimes education and explanation is needed. At other times, where this is not desired or would not be understood, the plan might need to be dropped or modified in favour of peace. This does not entail compromising your integrity. It entails adding the wisdom of a larger picture to it. Your chosen action or words may

indeed be true or helpful. But it may be that in the current situation they would not be received in this light and would therefore only cause trouble. To pursue them with this knowledge would hint that your intent comes from your ego rather than from wisdom and the desire for the greater good. Surrendering your idea in this light is a sign of strength not weakness, and of integrity not compliance. It is also about using timing to the advantage of the greater good.

3. Consider always, before responding, how the other will hear your words, or receive your action. It may be obvious to you what your intention is, but when you are at a higher frequency, others often cannot understand your intention as you meant it. Therefore you must be extra careful to be both clear and patient, as well as to quickly correct any misinterpretations. The onus is on you, – after all, you are the 'odd one out'! And besides, it is easier for you than for most, to understand all sides. This way you can nip many conflicts in the bud.

4. When you are sure of what you are about to do or say, spend one second passing it by your heart. Does it feel right? If it does, it is probably appropriate. If it does not, excuse yourself, have a toilet break or whatever to give yourself time, and think again. Perhaps you have overlooked something. Because of where you are coming from, your actions and words will affect others more than most, so you have a responsibility to be careful. Take this responsibility seriously. In so doing, you will be empowered to make a positive

difference to the world and all you meet.

Energy hygiene

Then remember too, to brush your teeth and wash your face, before you hit the streets! More obvious advice? Perhaps not so. You all know about dirt. But do not forget about psychic dirt – the 'stuff' you collect energetically as you make your way about your day. Because you are probably a healer, you might be more inclined than most to pick up others' energy garbage, without realising it. Dark is attracted to light, so in the course of a day you might pick up all sorts of dense vibrations, which can affect you adversely in a number of ways. They can have an affect emotionally, physically, mentally, or spiritually, and the worst of it is that you will probably think 'it is just me', and accept these changes when you do not need to. We do not necessarily advocate protecting yourself wherever you go. This can become a rather paranoid process. Rather be sure to have some sort of clearing routine which you embark on, say, before bedtime each night. Brush teeth, wash face, clear energy and into bed. That way you are assured of a more peaceful sleep too. There are many, many different ways to clear your energy. One simple way is to ask Archangel Michael to help you by removing from your energy field any adverse energy which is not yours. It is as simple as that. You do not need great manuals and long visualisations.

CHAPTER 11

Contradictions in terms

Contradictions abound in your beautiful world. It is like a patchwork of juxtapositions, inexplicable to each part within it. It is easier for us to see what is going on, being at something of a distance, compared to yourselves. So if you will allow us, we would like to share some more of our perceptions, in the hope they will add to your clarity. Mind you, we are not necessarily 'right'. That you will have to feel about and decide for yourselves. These are just our ways of seeing your dilemmas. Other beings from other places may well have different interpretations.

Your trail

We see you as very special individuals, each precious and unique and each bearing an errand from its soul. As you flit about, like angels, doing what you need to do, you leave a trail behind you. This trail carries the memory of all you are and have been and done. It stays there, where you have been, and forms the background for whatever happens there next. Now, along comes another angel-human, doing something no doubt important, and this one smells something odd. It is your trail. This second human has to contend with this trail, this memory pattern, as well as doing his job. This may not be easy. It may be a faint trail, or it may be a strong one. It may be one that fits with the second human, or it may be one which is contradictory and challenging. If it is both strong, and contradictory, the second human will encounter some difficulty maintaining his own patterns while endeavouring to accomplish his tasks. He might find himself picking up emotions he doesn't understand; having trouble concentrating; feeling aches and pains; or developing traits he never had before. When he leaves that place, he will then leave his own memory trail behind, which will be quite an accumulation of flavours by then. Imagine what the third human will have to encounter!

You are all dealing with these influences all the time. You go to the supermarket to pick up some cheese, and wonder why you return in a different frame of mind. You naturally assume this is due to something you know about, such as the traffic, the check-out queue or the increased prices. However, it is probably none of these things. By the time you have left the supermarket you have traversed the memory paths of hundreds, if not thousands of prior people, each of whom carry their personal history, worries, fears, happinesses and hopes. How can you possibly expect to go through all that unscathed? Some of these trails will have reinforced your existing state, some will have challenged it. No wonder shopping is tiring!

This will happen virtually wherever you go, because there is a history of people in most places on earth.

You are wondering what the relevance of all this is

to you? It is extremely relevant. Much of your power is lost to other times and people due to these unseen influences. If you are aware this is happening, you can learn to take steps to counteract these influences. There are many strategies which may help.

Dealing with unseen influences

Firstly, when you go out, remember to take with you your own angel, to protect you and guide you, at all times. All you have to do is ask. This is not craziness or wishful thinking. It is practicality, like taking your purse to the shop. This is what your angel likes to do, and it is a much-needed role to fulfil for you. Now, having done that, you already have some protection. The second step is to be sure about who you are and who you are not. If you find yourself developing some symptom, emotion, or trait that does not feel like you, do not adopt it and identify with it. Notice it as an anomaly, an intruder, and ask it to leave, as it does not belong to you. You can also consciously strengthen its opposite, so that it is weakened. For instance, if, after returning from a concert, you suddenly notice you are feeling inexplicably sad, ask the sadness to leave if it is not yours, and put on some cheerful music. If, after that you still feel sad, perhaps it is your sadness, which was roused from its unconscious state by the concert. If the sadness leaves you and doesn't return, it probably belonged to the woman sitting on your left, who recently lost her best friend to a car accident, or to the person who sat in your seat before you, who has to sell his house due to financial problems.

If you could see this, as we can, you would see many

little clouds of varied colours and brightness, and people moving in and out through them, changing them slightly as they go. Sometimes the clouds attach themselves to a person, and leave the place altogether, but this is rare. More often they interact, changing the cloud and the person's energy field.

It is now quite well-known that you can also powerfully change these little clouds by actually superimposing a cloud of your own. If you bring in white light, or pink light, this will dissipate negativity remarkably. This does not take any great skill. Once again, light concentration and firm intent will do the trick. Another popular method is to coat yourself in white light, before you venture into dubious places. This is effective too, as a barrier and a catalyst for change.

Before you go racing to a doctor, at the onset of sudden symptoms, be aware that they might not be yours. You could end up paying some stranger's doctor's bill! Especially if symptoms come upon you suddenly in a crowded place, a shop, or in a place where many people have been, suspect that you are being affected by place memory. Symptoms might be quite dramatic. No matter. Sit down if you need to, then before you race off for help, ask your angel to help, and ask the symptoms to leave if they are not yours. Very often, you will feel fine again within a minute or two.

Clearing your space

Naturally the place where you live will be subject to the memories you bring to it. If you are miserable on Sunday, but the cause of the misery has left by Monday, your recovery into happiness might be delayed by the memory of misery in your room. So having regular cleaning of the energy of your space is as important as brushing your teeth. Keep the space happy with music, clear it with the fire of candles or incense, the power of prayer, mantras or whatever technique you prefer. You will find books and courses on this topic.

The other point to bear in mind regarding this is the potential you have for power to actually help others through the trail you leave. If you are in balance, your trail will be strong and not easily diverted, and will have a positive effect upon later comers to the places you traverse. This is one of the ways in which your being in balance yourself helps the whole.

Money myths

Another thing we notice, from our vantage point, is the attitudes so many of you hold in relation to spending money. When you spend money, as an exchange for goods or services, you are putting out a small invitation to the universe, or the greater system, to fill a gap you have just created in your wallet. This is all very well and good. It makes the world go round, as you say. However, the problem is not so much in the spending, as in the receiving. For what will you receive in exchange for your money? It will ultimately be someone else's time and efforts, for this is what goods and services are made of. Now, you have given your money, received the time and efforts of someone else, and what then ensues? As you have said, the world then goes round. You must then expend more time and effort to accrue more money to balance the lack in your purse, to fill the hole created. Right? No, it does not work like that. What actually ideally then happens is that you wait, until you need something, and the need is filled or the money then appears somehow. That is how the flow naturally happens. However few of you let it happen that way. Instead you trust that you cannot trust the universe to supply your needs, and you battle it out to supply yourself with money, long before you actually need it. When you do this you are causing yourself a struggle, for you are going against the flow of the natural order. Having lots of money you do not need creates an imbalance. If you pour more water into the jug than its capacity, what happens? It runs all over the table, and down onto the floor, forming a puddle in which you might slip. Many people live in this way, unaware there is any other.

The Universal Banking System

Those who live with the flow, according to the needs of reasonable intent find they are well-supported, often in surprising and timely ways. Less effort is usually involved, yet they find they are able to get what they need.

So consider trusting in the Universal Banking System – perhaps open an account. This doesn't mean giving up your job, not yet anyway! It just means being a little more open to receiving what you need when you need it, instead of assuming you have to battle the forces of finance to make ends meet. It means not worrying when money is low, knowing your needs will be provided for in some other way. This attitude will allow that to be the case, and not block the flow.

Freedom from habit

A third contradiction between how we see things, and your experience of them, regards habits. This is indeed an unfortunate word, set as it is, in concrete. When you have a habit, it is part of your make-up. This must be so, because this is what the word means! But it is not so. A habit is merely a track you have travelled on many times before. It is not the only track for you, and you have not necessarily developed a flat tyre and got stuck on this track. Whoever coined this word did humanity a grave disservice, and greatly denied the flawlessness of your flexibility. Just because you have eaten a sandwich for lunch every day for five years, must you necessarily have one daily for the next five? Of course not. Choice is yours in every moment, and let no-one or word take that away from you. Each moment is a new one, completely fresh out of the box. Yes, you may impose some memories upon it, but you may also gild it with new thought, and expose it to the rays of today's sun. It is nonsense to suppose that because you have done a certain thing numerous times, you are trapped in a never-ending cycle of addiction to this behaviour! This is psychobabble at its best! The statisticians among you know that if you toss a coin, even if heads comes up 5 times in a row, the chances of tails on the next toss remains 50%. Each toss is independent of all the others. In the same way, you are free to choose your next moment, regardless of your last. Do not use the word 'habit' as an excuse to remain the same, when you know change is due. It is only a servant of procrastination, when used this way, and has mastery over you, instead of vice versa.

Once you have made a clear decision, it is easy to see how meaningless that word 'habit' really is. Usually it is used as an excuse when the mind is not yet clear and the intent is feeble.

So enjoy exercising your freedom, and let no mere words curtail you.

CHAPTER 12

Opening up to a new reality

Before you build sandcastles you must wet the sand, or it will crumble back into a shapeless pile. So it is with your own reality. There must be an agent to help it cohere. We will explain: When your current reality has become outdated, and it is time for a new one to be formed in your life, this new one must have something to latch on to, in order to be sustained. Now there are two points to understand here. Firstly, the 'new' reality will not actually be new at all – it will merely be uncovered, or discovered. It has been there all along, but your blindfolds would not allow you access to it. Secondly, unless you avail yourself of the opportunity to perceive afresh, this 'new' reality will fade back into your background and again become obscure, like the collapsed sandcastle. So the new reality, in a sense, must find fertile ground in your conscious being, to grow and prosper.

This may sound rather mystifying to most of you, who have not yet reached this stage. It is information you may need later, and later it may make more sense.

Dropping the Blindfold

As you develop through the many experiences you create for yourselves, you will gradually be unravelling your blindfolds and seeing more of what is. This will happen to you all, as this is the evolutionary stage you have now reached. However, in order to sustain the gains you make, you will need certain attributes, otherwise you may well find yourselves slipping back and going round in unnecessary circles. These attributes will be the water in the sandcastle of your new reality. Let us examine them.

Openness

The first one is openness. Circumstances may conspire to give you a glimpse of reality from time to time, but unless you have an open attitude, you will not be able to hold onto these glimpses for long, for your old patterns will insist on re-establishing themselves. An open attitude means an attitude based in the present, not the past. It means an attitude which sees clearly without judging; which is flexible enough to re-align and learn without resistance. An open attitude is one devoid of fixed expectations, which are limiting. An open attitude is one open both to circumstances, and to yourself and your potential. If you see yourself as limited, you may be unable to integrate the new less limited vision of reality into your life, and may cause yourself so much conflict that you eventually sacrifice the vision for the sake of peace.

Trust

The second type of water needed for your sandcastle

is trust. We have not yet spoken of trust, but it is one of the most desirable traits for you to develop, as you will need it always in the coming days – even more than you have needed it in the past. Trust involves a certain surrender; a giving up of the notion of having complete control. It means allowing destiny to take its course without too much interference, and certainly without worry. Trust, like openness, must be directed towards the self as well as the outer circumstances, for it to be useful. To trust is to know that all will be well, regardless of how things seem at the time. This is ultimately always so, in the greater scheme of things.

Allowance

Then third, is allowance, which is allied to trust, but subtly different. Allowance is the ability to respond with generosity and understanding to situations and people, so that freedom is fostered around you. Both allowance and trust create fertile grounds for unlimitedness, and they are the death knell for limitation.

If you are open, trusting and allowing, your new visions of reality will fall on fertile grounds, and your blindfolds will continue to unravel.

CHAPTER 13

Tumbling into the unknown

When you are about to embark upon a new career, you usually do a little research. You find out what will be expected of you, and check that you have the qualifications or experience needed. This research may be basically done in two different ways. Either it will be exact and defined, or it will be flexible and fluid. Let us explain ourselves:

Say you are contemplating a job as a secretary. The exact method of research would have you asking whether you have been a secretary before or whether you have completed a secretarial course. The flexible method would have you asking whether you have the potential to be a secretary; whether you are capable of learning the skills required. The difference between the two methods is in the level of limitation implied in the outcome. The exact method would produce rigid 'yes/no' answers. The flexible method would lead to far more 'maybe's'. The flexible method would therefore be more inclusive, and give more options.

Feeling your way

In your coming days you will be faced with many new situations, requiring decision-making, and perhaps some prior research. You will be changing so much that to base your research on the exact method would be unnecessarily limiting. You may well be heading for situations that you have never previously encountered. This does not mean you will not have the potential to meet the challenges. It is largely your flexibility and openness which will qualify you.

Soon you will probably find that, in fact, no method of research is the right one; that the way to know how to proceed is merely to notice what feels right. All the other factors will become fairly irrelevant as you grow into your unlimited state. You will find you are able to roll with your chosen destiny, a bit like a tumbler in a circus, without getting hurt. Only when something goes strongly against your grain will you need to stop and re-evaluate, and perhaps slightly change direction.

Flow

At no point will you need to resist anything in your life, as this only causes effort and pain. Instead you will roll with it, and when it does not feel right, you will keep rolling towards what does feel right. 'Feel right' does not mean right in relation to the norms of society, or even your religions. It means feeling right within yourself. This produces a sense of peace and congruence. As soon as you feel incongruent or fragmented in some way, you will know a change of direction is needed. This way of life is one few of you now follow, and it is the most effortless and efficient of all.

Faith

Sometimes you may ask yourself whether you were meant to be in a certain situation in which you find yourself. Remember, you are always meant to be exactly where you are. Knowing this is part of the trick of non-resistance. If you know this, you will be better able to accept where you are and move from there, rather than being stuck questioning and doubting. Questioning is only useful if it produces a fairly quick answer. After that, it becomes a waste of your energy. Doubting is never useful, but it is a symptom of lack of understanding. If you can bypass understanding, and instead accept, in the deep sense of the word, you will not need to doubt. This sort of acceptance is called faith. It has been said that with faith mountains can be moved. This is true. One of the reasons is that no energy is wasted. It is all directed to the task at hand.

CHAPTER 14

Tomorrow

Unlike us, you are not fully aware of your motives and reasons. Motives are strange things - they hook onto your actions and bend them this way and that, without you even knowing they are there. Understanding your own motives is quite an art. As you know, arts can be learned, and this art is within the reach of anyone who really wants it. There are certain steps to be followed.

Until humanity has understood today clearly, there can be no clear tomorrow.

Unconscious motives

If you wish to understand your motives – the things that propel you forward, and sometimes land you in tight spots – you need to begin at the beginning. This entails looking carefully at where you have come from, in order to begin at your particular starting block. So often you seem to take it for granted that the whole human race starts from the same starting block. This could not be further from the truth. Remember, you have each had many, many lives before, and come into this one with your own little suitcase of fears, assumptions, prejudices, wishes, goals, blinkers and so on. None of them are right or wrong – they just are.

So here we have this little planet, full of people holding little invisible suitcases, containing all manner of contents. When these people speak, or think or act, the jack-in-the-box all too often pops out of the suitcases, and does the speaking, thinking or acting for them, before they've had time to realize it! What a circus! Then the person on the receiving end responds to the owner of the suitcase via the contents of his own suitcase – and soon neither of them know what is going on. The minds become confused, the communication misses the mark, and a new set of data is added to the suitcase. All very chaotic!

The only way out of this trap of confusion and blindness is to sit down in an undisturbed place, open the suitcase, and investigate its contents. 'Not always easy', you might say. 'Too busy, too distressing, too hard.' Well, it depends: what are you willing to sacrifice in order to really own yourself? As long as you carry that suitcase, you are a slave to its contents. Once you have stared deeply into its contents, you will find they have vanished, and you have both arms free.

Finding patterns

'How do I look into the suitcase anyway?' you ask. It is not difficult. It is about patterns. What you have in your little case is really a pattern book – which knits you in certain ways throughout life. Once you are aware it is about patterns, you can start finding yours. Some people follow a pattern of brutality – whatever obstacle seems to stand in their way, they crush it, one way or another. Some follow a pattern of being a victim – time after time they feel powerless and over-ruled. Some are only comfortable if busy – to be still means that unpleasant feelings surface, and this feels dangerous. Some are laissez-faire, easy come, easy go, unruffled in the most trying of situations. Some seek and seek, but are afraid of finding. Some must be leaders, others must be followers. Some respond to any new situation with fear and apprehension, while others lap up new opportunities as a way of proving themselves. Some feel as though they will die if criticised; others appreciate the opportunity to learn. The key to knowing what you hold in your suitcase is that it will manifest in your life again and again. It will be your fall-back position.

Releasing

Now, as we have said, none of these patterns is bad. Each pattern is a learned response, sensibly chosen by you at some stage in your many lives. Each pattern is ultimately a survival technique, to enable you to adapt to tricky times. However, the problem is that, once those particular times are gone, the pattern lingers on, and is no longer useful. It then becomes a hindrance, limiting your responses to life.

If you wish to be rid of all this, then ask. Basically that is all it takes. There are now so many beings helping you to evolve, that, whereas years ago you would have needed years of psychotherapy, now, all you need do is ask. With asking, of course, goes allowing. You will need to allow your old patterns to drop from you, in order to adopt freedom. It is no good asking to be rid of your fears, then continuing to cling to them, as they offer you a way of avoiding responsibility. Allowing your old patterns to be released requires courage. Sometimes it is the courage of stepping into the void – the 'dark night of the soul', as you call it. Because, once the props of who you seemed to be are removed, you may wonder what is left, and who you now are. There may be many nights of weeping and gnashing of teeth! But finally, you will discover yourself for the first time, all shiny new and squeaky clean. And with absolutely no suitcase to carry. This, as you will discover, is a good feeling. It is the springboard to infinity.

The perfect future

From this springboard, you can build a perfect future – one unlimited by preconceptions, boundaries and fears. What do we mean by 'a perfect future'? We hear you, already limiting this concept. 'There is no such thing as perfect.' 'Too idealistic.' 'Impossible.'

But it is possible. You can have everything in your life exactly as you wish it. Provided you empty that suitcase. If you fully emptied it, you would be fully aware. If you were fully aware, you would be powerful enough to create in your world a mirror of your ideal.

For the first time in your history, this option is available to ordinary (a silly word, as none of you are ordinary!) people. Previously only a select few could attain this status, but now, as we have reiterated, you have much help. All we need is your intent, and request. We cannot say that this emptying of your suitcase would happen overnight. This would be rare. Instead, with your steady intent, you would be guided to discover and release your patterns, over time. In direct proportion to how much you allow this release, you will experience an increase of power and freedom. Once you are used to these, joy follows.

Fear of power

Initially there will be many of you who will sabotage this process, as part of your baggage will consist of a fear of power. You have been powerful before, and it has not led to happy events. Release, release. It is the only way to move forward. Times have changed. This is the time to regain that power.

Movement and stillness

As we mentioned earlier, in your assorted tomorrows there will be much movement. Movement towards and movement away from. The only way to manage such a degree of movement easily is by not being too attached to your surroundings. Move lightly, letting go of your past as you head forward. This past includes relationships, possessions, places and items. Take with you only your soul and the bare essentials. This is all you'll need. When there is much movement, people often panic and become lost in the hustle and bustle. So, at the time of most movement, you will need to create the most inner stillness, to compensate and keep you focussed. This is not difficult, if you have become a friend of stillness, but may indeed be difficult, if you have not encountered it before. So we suggest a little practise would be in order.

The order of change

Order sets about trying to define chaos as best it can. However, in your world there is already an order, which mankind does not fully comprehend. This order goes something like this: first there is energy, then there is will, then there is action or change. This is always the order leading to change. The forthcoming changes in your world follow the same pattern, so it is pointless trying to stop them, through any means at all. The energy and the will for the changes have been set in place, and happen they will. However, the third part of the order does rest with man. That is to do with the quality of the movement during the change. As we have discussed, this is where mankind can make a big difference. So focus your attention on the manner in which you will move with the changes, not on trying to stop them.

Whatever you do, will be of little consequence in the long term, except to you yourself. Remember, it is the journey of your own soul you are responsible for, and ultimately nothing else.

CHAPTER 15

On Light

Light and love, as we have mentioned before, are related. What is their relationship? Light instantly transforms darkness into itself, as long as it is present. Love binds, holds together, unites, links, joins. Therefore love is a creative force. For what is creation but the opposite of destruction, which is a pulling apart? Creation is the making of something, which implies the formation of thought or matter into various patterns. Love was, in fact, the basis of all creation. This love then split into light and dark. Each was there to complement and balance the other. Together they formed a whole. Together they formed love.

Polarities

For creation to get any further this initial split needed to happen. This split then automatically created other splits. Opposites needed to be formed to create a dynamism, which would engender the movement of energy. These opposites, or polarities would forever seek to be re-united. This quest would form the basis of much of the motivation of life on Earth and in all other places.

Light forms the staple for much of life on your Earth. It is needed by plants and animals, birds and fish. This is the obvious side of light, taught to your children in schools. Then there is the other side of light – the light of consciousness. This is less well-known.

The light of consciousness

Each of you actually has two selves: a light self and a dark one. This may come as something of a surprise for you, as your scientists have not yet spotted this under a microscope! Your quest throughout your lives has always been to unite these two selves. Once these are united fully, the dark self merges into the light self and is no longer. Instead you have reformed into the original love of which you were made. You are then one with all creation, and at peace. Everything you humans have done on Earth has symbolically reflected this struggle of yours to re-unite the dark with the light. In order to have some definition, you have judged the dark 'bad' and the light 'good'. Well, you wisely chose to identify with the winning side! However, it would have been easier for you had you not made this distinction at all, because in doing so you created judgement. We will not get distracted into a discussion about judgement here. Suffice it to say this has been one of the bigger detours for humanity. Humanity as a whole is now coming close to re-uniting its darkness with its light; and so is each of you. However, much negativity has been placed on the darkness, through man's judgement.

The merging

As the light shines on the darkness in the beginning stages of their merging, this negativity becomes very apparent. This is what is happening currently on your Earth. All sorts of unpleasantness is coming to light, literally. Man is witnessing how ugly he can be, how destructive he can be, how sick he has made his environment, and many other anomalies. It is a time to witness, act out and then release all of the darkness into the light. In a way, the worse things appear to get, the more brightly the light must be shining. Remember this.

So, when all is light, all will be love. The darkness will have merged into the light, and there will be perfect peace. This is what we have spoken of as paradise. There are many ways to explain the same thing. This cycle of re-uniting entails a cleansing, and this is what the Earth, too is experiencing.

RIDING THE CHANGE

CHAPTER 16

Diving into Darkness

Do not be afraid of the dark. The dark is only a convolution of the light – in a sense, a shadow of the light. It is not a separate entity, for nothing is, in effect, separate.

We would tell you a little about darkness, for it is given so much space, in your minds and in your media.

The darkness is a friend. It is the way you can measure the light. Without it you would have known no contrast and no joy. The problems occur when the ratio becomes unbalanced. There is meant to be more light than dark, the dark merely forming a backdrop and a perspective for the light. However humans have fed the dark so much with fear, that it has become a monstrous part of your lives, claiming victims emotionally, mentally, physically and spiritually. Had humanity remembered its connection with the light, this would not have been able to eventuate. However, when you feel lost, even the slightest 'bump in the night' frightens you.

Apparently dark actions

Some of the dark action that takes place in your

world could only be described as evil experiments by misguided individuals or groups, who have lost their way. Other events, which appear to have dark roots, may actually be a part of the shattering of your current illusory reality. This has to be done, and at times dark forces are harnessed to do it. The collective consciousness of mankind uses beings only too happy to destroy, to do the necessary job. This is one of the reasons people will be confused about who are the 'angels' and who are the 'demons' in your future world events. The darkness must act itself out, and the light will come up to meet it, and eventually triumph. Of that there is no doubt.

What to do... or be

However, many of you will wonder what to do at these times of crisis. There is a simple answer to this question: nothing. Do nothing at all. This means being – for when you are not doing, you are just being. And when you are fully just being, you are able to connect with love – the force of unity. Love and power, are closely associated. If you tap into love, through stillness, you are tapping into power. Your external reality mirrors your internal one, so the more you tap into the power of love, the more that will be represented in your outer reality. If, on the other hand, you tap into hatred, anger and vengeance, this is what you will be creating in your world. 'But', you say 'we can't stand by and watch atrocities happening, and do nothing!' We understand your concerns, and your very human need to do something to change the scenario, but this has never worked very well. You have never really tried this alternative, so you have no idea of how it would work.

Diplomacy has failed, to a large extent, in your world. It has been useful in many cases, but in the larger scheme of things, it has not been used to bring about balance and equity. War certainly has not worked. It may have appeared to end certain power struggles, but it has left so much damage, on all levels. What other options have you tried? From where we are, we see a riveting vacuum in your ideas about this. So, when someone hits you, you hit him back, or you attempt to talk him out of hitting you again, or perhaps you run away. These are not the only ways. Some of your religions have taught you to 'turn the other cheek'. This was not meant as an invitation for the abuser to hit you yet again, but for you to collect yourself and get into a space of love, which will ricochet back to the abuser. When people are in the vibration of love, they do not abuse others. The fear is 'but if I turn my back and do nothing, he will hit me again and again.' It does not work this way. One of the few people in history who successfully loved his persecutors was Jesus Christ. His influence has been carried forward for 2000 years. That is power! If you wanted to interpret that event in terms of winners and losers, clearly Jesus won and his persecutors lost. His body may have died, but his spirit certainly did not; whereas the instigators of his death have left no legacy of their own.

Dealing with abuse

We do understand that there is much fear

surrounding such a concept. All the 'what if's'! Perhaps it would be worth trying it out at home first, in your family situations, where you feel fairly safe. When something slightly abusive happens to you – speech or action – become calm and centred, and focus on love. See what happens next. We bet the wind will be taken out of your abuser's sails! If you refuse to 'rise to the occasion', it is left to the abuser to react to her own action. It is rare she will do the same thing twice. Usually the abuser will instead be forced to stop and reassess the effectiveness of her abuse, as it has not elicited the desired response of fear, anger, retaliation and so on. Abusers often like retaliation, because this allows them the excuse to continue the abuse, often at an escalated level. Remember, abuse is usually a move in a game, played by people who feel as though they are already losing and haven't got much more to lose. If you give them love, instantly they have something to lose by continuing to abuse you. Everyone, every single person, actually wants love. There is a deep level at which you know your survival depends upon it.

Now please do not misunderstand us. We are not telling you to stand by and watch the abuse or misfortunes of others. Run to their aid, do all you can to help them, but do not waste energy on retaliation towards their attackers. Stop the attackers by all means, if you can do so without escalating the abuse. It is a loving action to help someone back to natural behaviour. This does not mean we condone violence. We do not like it nor do we practise it. But in your world it is a reality at this stage, and one you need to learn to deal with more effectively. Some religions have recommended 'forgiving' those who attack you. The point of this is not to 'be nice', or a 'good person'. The point is that by being in a state of love, it is you who will have the power. You will have released yourself from the bondage of hatred, fear and anger, which cut you off from your true power. Light is always more powerful than dark. Short term this may require much courage, but in the longer term, it is the only way to solve the problems of your world.

The battle is on

There is, of course, another way of looking at all this. That is through the telescope. If one looks as from a distance, one is able to see a greater pattern being played out here. It is the battle of light and dark. For there is now such a battle, which has been brought into being through the imbalance of your world, and the necessity of the times. It is a crucial battle upon which much hangs. Whether or not you will be involved in the battle is not the question. Each moment, each one of you is playing a role in the battle, one way or the other. So be aware of what you are supporting. You wouldn't want to be barracking inadvertently for the wrong team, would you? All your thoughts, words and actions count – they all create either light or dark. The more light you create now, the quicker the battle will be over, and the less damage will have been done. This is no 'airy-fairy' advice. It is as real as the letters you are reading, and will later be better understood by your science, which is fast discovering many secrets.

Growth opportunities

It is often said that you never hurt as badly as when you have been wounded by one of your own. The reason this is true is because of a loss of trust. You expect those close to you to be worthy of your trust, and when they prove to be otherwise, it may shake you to the core and rock your very foundations. This can leave you open to doubting everything around you. It is not a happy position, but it is one in which can set the stage for much growth. It is a state which shatters illusions, and can therefore open you up to a totally new way of looking at reality. So, if this happens to you in the coming times of great change, use the opportunity for growth wisely. Do not get stuck in the negativity of the emotions, but move on to new perceptions, after the time of shock is over. Allow yourself fresh visions of your surrounding society and world. These may be just the visions you have needed for a long time, which were blocked from your perception by out-dated assumptions.

Looking through the telescope

Remember: although change may come suddenly, violently and apparently unasked for, it may be very needed. Allow yourself to roll with the punches of your times, and within the roll, to seek out the later benefits of the change. Many events will take place in your world which may appear all bad, all destructive, but will facilitate constructive change. This is the time to step back, get out the telescope, and have a good look from a long distance away. Grieve, yes, mourn, yes, but then move on and move into the changed time with a changed outlook. This is the way your world will progress rapidly, which it now must.

Remember, it is all to help you find the best route to paradise on your tram.

Envisioning the Light

Dark times are times in which there is the most potential for love. Unity is needed to change the darkness into light. One person in the dark is less likely to find the light switch than a whole group of you! So get together and bolster up each other's capacity for spreading light, through talking about what you envision, not what you fear. It is never a good idea to spread fear, although easily accomplished. Fear of the dark only magnifies its power. Love of the dark turns it into a harmless friend. If you shine a torch into the darkness, what happens? It is no longer darkness – where the torchlight strikes it, it has become light. This is how it works. Very simple.

Choosing freely

Another matter to be mentioned is the one of retribution, as though someone is keeping score. 'Because you have been mean to me, I cannot be your friend'. When you adopt this attitude, you are giving away your power. You are allowing the other's action to dictate your response. Would you curtail your own freedom in this way? At any time you have the right to decide what action to take, from an infinite range of possibilities. You are never forced to respond in a certain way, by another's action towards you. Allow yourself the freedom of real choice before you choose your words and actions. Let the assumptions, conditioning and societal cliches sink to the bottom of the lake and then look carefully into the clear waters of choice. This way you will be laying the foundation stone of a freer and more creative future.

CHAPTER 17

Dancing to the Tune of the Universe

Has it ever struck you how indifferent most people are to what befalls others in their midst? There is a moment's pause in routine, to watch the news, or offer sympathy, then the routine goes on unchanged. How is this so? Is there not some imbalance indicated somewhere, when a person or persons create the need to suffer? You would probably agree, but the link between you and this fact may seem obscure. Remember, you are a tiny part of a giant hologram and all aspects of your world and universes are strongly interlinked. If one part is out of balance, so are all parts. If one part suffers, all suffer. To deny this is to live in fantasy. Therefore, when you see or hear of someone, or something, in distress, there are many implications.

The world as mirror

Firstly, the fact that this knowledge has reached you means it is part of your personal world. This means the distress must be a part of you too. So, now we have someone else in distress, and the understanding that you must be distressed also at some level. Believe us, this is how it works – a giant mirror. Of course you may choose to ignore both pieces of information – deny the inner and outer distress, and get on with the job as usual. This would be tricky, but possible in the short term. The later result of this tactic will usually be greater and more hard-hitting inner and outer distress. Another choice would be to tut-tut for a while about the other's distress, send flowers or indicate support in some other way, or actually do something to help the other's situation – a donation to an aid agency for example. These are all very nice, and may make you feel better and feel you have done something, but they won't ultimately change the problem, which is imbalance. The third option is to recognise the distress as a mirror of your own inner distress and do something to rectify this. You may also wish to help the other party, but the important thing is to recognise the distress is yours, therefore the responsibility to fix it lies with you. This inner part is also the part you have more control over. You cannot really change another person, but you always have the choice and power to change yourself. If you do, as a consequence, the other may well change.

The symbolism of natural disasters

So, let us return to our dilemma. You have just read again about a disaster on the other side of the world, where many people are perishing in floods, fires or earthquakes. You feel sad for them, and helpless. What can you do against forces like this? The answer, as usual, is nothing. Those forces are doing what they need to do: cleansing the earth, stirring people's compassion, allowing people to fulfil their destinies. What can you do to help, and to ensure less of this sort of suffering has to happen in future?

Perhaps send money, but primarily, seek to find the imbalance within yourself, which is causing a part of you to suffer, and which would necessitate cleansing and re-balancing.

Look to the symbolism of what has happened for clues. Floods are to do with water. Water is often symbolic of the emotions, and floods are an excess, like tears. Floods ultimately have a cleansing function, but in the acute stages, dangerous debris may be swirling all around, and much muck may be stirred up. Earthquakes, on the other hand, are a result of faults – cracks in the earth, pressures and shifts which upset balance and stability. The very foundation upon which you rest is shaken up and reset, by a quake. Volcanoes erupting bring forth the very essence of power of the earth. They declare 'Look – I am not to be meddled with.' That fierce power and heat has bubbled and boiled underneath the surface sometimes for hundreds of years, but the time has come for a release. The imbalance of the internal and external is too great to contain it any longer. Hurricanes, tornadoes and other destructive wind related phenomena are about change. They sweep clean whatever is in their path. They are about endings and beginnings. Only that which is truly flexible survives. All else is broken and snapped. The hurricane is a leveller. What has been built up is levelled to the ground, so new starts may be made. Fires, like water, are cleansing, but they have a different flavour. The flavour of burning is one of ferocity and power, similar to the volcano. The fire may be merciless and all-consuming, but it leaves a quietness in its wake. From this quietness, contemplation may feed new attitudes and new beginnings. Violence among people speaks of a loss of connection and a consequent desperation. It is the most severely unnatural behaviour of all, and betokens a loss of connection with the natural world and with man's true nature.

Finding balance

Remember, you are like a mini replica of the whole earth. You have a core of raw power; you rest upon a foundation of beliefs, ideals, assumptions, experiences; you contain numerous people within your personality, all jockeying for position; you are threaded to eternity by a soul which precedes you in this life, and will outlive you; you reach out of yourself into the other aspects of the world through your thought, activities and speech. Imbalance can occur in most of these aspects of you, and in their relationships to each other. When it does, this imbalance will be mirrored in your outer world. Seeing it there affords you an opportunity to recognise it and correct it.

For instance, you might read about a war in which humans are butchering other humans. This is most unnatural, and indicates something unnatural is happening in you too. On self-examination, you might find there is an aspect of you that you are not accepting – you are trying to kill that part of yourself which wants to 'be lazy', by being a workaholic. That part of you which is craving a rest is being violated.

Now, were you to recognised its validity, and decide not only to take a holiday, but to respect it as an ongoing part of your life, and work shorter hours, you would be creating new harmony between some aspects of your inner being. We are not saying this would cause a truce on the other side of the world, but it would be a strong step in the right direction. It would also probably improve your health and feelings of well-being. But it might mean changing some assumptions, and would certainly involve being less judgemental and more accepting.

Willing helpers

You are complex beings. It is easy for you to become out of balance, as you are pulled and pushed by a huge number of factors in your world. The more out of balance you are, the more out of balance your world is. All the emails, protest marches, donations and petitions will have less effect than you quietly finding your own balance. This is where your power lies in changing your world.

Now, you may be thinking you need to qualify as a psychotherapist before you are able to work yourself out to this extent! This is where the universe comes in. You already have many, many unseen 'psychotherapists', who can help you on your way, provided you are willing. Your part of the deal is to recognise that you operate in concert with the rest of the earth; that there is a problem which you therefore own; and that you wish to rectify this problem. The more you understand about what the problem is, the better. But this is not entirely necessary. It is your intent which carries the most power. Thought and will always precedes action and change. So, once you have thrown this intent out into the universe, there are unseen helpers who will catch it, and make the changes you seek manifest themselves, as long as you allow this.

This is one process you can follow to bring peace to yourself and your world.

Energies of city and desert

If you were to look at your world from high up in space, you would see clusters where many humans live – your cities. Here there is a great density, not only of population, but of energy. The 'molecules' of energy are closer together, more tightly packed, compared to those in, say, a desert. This being the case, there is more potential for intensity, because each of those 'molecules' carries a charge. This charge is there, waiting to be directed by human thought, speech or action.

Now imagine all the thought, speech and action that takes place daily in one of your cities. It is a powerful combination of influences, which brings to bear all sorts of effects on your lives. Some of these influences lead towards happy balance, some away.

What we see is a collection of energies, moving and shifting with great dynamism. Each shift leaves an alteration in the pattern of the whole, which then forms the basis for the next shift.

In the desert, and other more uninhabited places, it looks very different. The shifts initiated here are slower, and each one is more effective, because there are fewer of them. However, patterns do not necessarily change as easily here. They may revert to what they were for centuries, after a small shift. In the cities change proceeds rapidly and there is seldom reversal to past patterns.

What is the relevance of all this to you? Well, there are several points to be aware of.

Keeping the balance

Firstly, you now understand that the whole always has to be in balance. So a great deal of intensity in one area necessitates quietness in another. This means, the more you concentrate your busyness in cities, the more you are creating other places where there will have to be destruction to counter the construction; horizontal space to counter the vertical planes; stagnation to counter the changes; delays to counter the speed; and barrenness to counter the life. So your cities are effectively causing more desert; causing farmers to fail; causing the downfall of forests; causing salinity and barrenness in the land; causing small towns to live in poverty and disrepair. Strange, but true. The balance must be kept, in the microcosm, and in the macrocosm. It is not always a healthy balance, but balance it will be, for that is the way of nature.

Of course the corollary follows. If you were to bring more dynamism, growth and life to the quiet areas, the cities would slow a little. Would this not create a happier balance than the one you now have, in which most city people are moving at dizzying pace, and many country people are 'going under'?

We are not suggesting turning your national parks into development sites. We are suggesting injecting a little more investment of energy, thought, money and time into your small towns and empty spaces. This would help balance the intensity of your cities, probably leading to lower rates of crime, depression, drug abuse and other signs of alarm.

The problem is that the link between city and country is not understood. Each is seen as needy in its own right, and in competition with the other. But there never was a competition. There has always been co-operation, at the energy level, which is the basis of all manifestation.

Balancing from the inside

Now most of you are not town planners, mayors, politicians or economists, and wonder what you can do about this. It is very simple. You can all make a difference. Balance the busyness of the cities from within, by balancing your own busyness. We have talked about this before, and we will do so again. Bring stillness into your life and you will be helping the cities and the country. Set aside times of contemplation or meditation, if you do not wish to slow down generally. This may seem an obscure way to change such a huge balance problem, but it is actually very direct and immediate.

Let us remind you of your power, once again – you who often feel so overwhelmed at the state of the world. There is much you can do, and much you can salvage. It is simple. You created it and you can change it, with a little more understanding. Just remember that your every thought and action affects the whole, very literally.

Contagion and conformity

Another repercussion of the intensity in cities is the potential for contagion. As people, energy 'molecules', thoughts and actions are so closely packed, there is much infection, hence conformity. This is how the term 'political correctness' came into being. What it means is 'fitting the mould of the group'. It is more difficult to be an individual in a city than in a loosely-packed country community. In the cities those who feel themselves to be different often move in packs, live in the same areas, and dress similarly. Whereas in the country, they tend to be alone, and to express themselves uniquely. Here there is less group pressure. Therefore to be truly free and a master of your destiny, takes more strength in a city, than it would in an isolated place, where norms are less set, and there is more space for differences. It also has more effect than it would have in the country. So, if you can learn to be yourself within the busyness and madness of a city, you are creating a new pattern, which will serve others who may travel in your wake. Within the intensity of a city it is easy to become lost – to be carried away by the collective flow. Extra consciousness is needed to remain ahead and above this, and be able to see where you are going clearly, despite the pull around you. This is a little easier in the country, where the slower pace, and greater space allows for a more unimpeded view of the path.

We are not judging either the cities or the country

to be 'better'. We are merely pointing out a few ways you can create a more harmonious situation for all concerned, with, ultimately, less suffering.

The need for gardens

Your gardens and parks are spaces that help to balance the intensity of your cities. The more these are turned into building sites, the harder it will be for all of you, in both city and country, for the balance must be maintained. If space is removed from the cities, it must be regained elsewhere somehow. You can help by ensuring your own home is a place of peace, or that at least one area of it is dedicated to this. And consider the importance of keeping your garden, rather than adding on multiple rooms.

Work and leisure

It is similar with your employment situation. The more some work long hours, the more others must be unemployed. This even your mathematics can work out. But it is not just the working hours. It is also the fact that these people are creating an imbalance in their lives of too much work and not enough leisure. So others must have little work and much leisure to correct this balance. You can help by ensuring you maintain a balance in your own life.

Opportunities of city and country

The intensity of a city may provide a wonderful fishbowl of opportunities for growth, if it is encountered wisely. Here you may choose almost any experience, and see how you come up to meet it.

You can also pit your integrity against the flow of the collective, and thus test your mettle. But it may be a trap for the unwary, who may well find themselves drowning in collective folly.

The country, on the other hand, offers opportunity for quieter self-discovery; for self-reliance and the acceptance of differences; for contact with nature and the internalisation of space. It may be a trap for the stuck, who may not find enough impetus for change.

Each has its advantages, and each relies upon the other.

CHAPTER 18

Up the Spiral Staircase

At the end of your long tram ride home, there will be a spiral staircase, which you will need to climb to reach the front door. Then you will grasp the handle, turn the knob, and find yourself in a brand new world. Miraculous it will be indeed, and splendid. 'But when?', you ask, 'when will this all happen?' No-one knows this, as there is still much uncertainty, and free will abounds. So be patient.

Climbing the staircase

Meanwhile, we will give you some clues about how to climb this staircase. Firstly, this staircase has a silver rail, for you to hold on to, so you cannot fall. The rail is made of certainty. This is the certainty born of determination. Grasp it tightly, and it will help you find your way from step to step. Between each step is a gap, through which you can see the world turning. Do not focus on this movement, as you may become distracted. Keep your eye on the step you wish to reach. This way your success will be assured. The steps, too are silver, shiny and reflective. In them you may see the images of many things, but do not let this bother you. Let these images whirl past if they must, and keep your focus on the step above. Gradually you will find yourself going up further until you sense a detachment from the earth, and a connection with something greater. Then you know you are close to the door. Some will find the door to be oaken and heavy, others will find it already open. When you are there, you will know what to do.

Raising vibrations

We are speaking, of course, about the raising of your vibrations, to allow you access to paradise. This may seem an elusive process – hard to grasp, and even harder to accomplish. But, please know this has been happening for many years now, and you are already a long way up. It is only the last part you will have to do alone – the walking through the door. The rest of the way you are receiving much help.

When it is time for you to walk alone, you will be ready for this. In the meantime we have some tips, which may help you to climb your staircase with confidence.

1. As you ascend along life's path of trials and tribulations, you may find yourself a little baffled at times. 'What', you may ask, 'is the meaning of all this? Why am I going through this?' At these times it is more important for you to keep more focussed on where you are going, than on finding the answer to your question. Searching for an answer may waste years of valuable time, peace of mind, attention to the tasks at hand, and the ability to focus on the moment. In terms of your journey up the staircase, it may be like being fixated on one

step, instead of moving gracefully on. The answer is not as important as the way you deal with the situation, and what you learn from it. These will help you onto the next step. This does not mean we are advocating blindness or lack of insight. No, it is helpful to seek the meaning in your experiences, but when this meaning is not readily forthcoming, let the search go, and move on.

2. As you move on, you will find that your footsteps become lighter, your vision becomes clearer and your gaze stretches further. This is because you will be entering a different vibratory field, in which your impact will be changed. It is nothing to do with your intention. It is merely to do with the scenery through which you will be travelling. When you travel in a car, the scenery seems to become more blurred as you drive faster. When you slow down, it all comes back into focus. When you are further up the staircase, at a higher frequency, the atmosphere will be offering you less resistance, so you will feel lighter and more 'floaty', and be able to see further, after, perhaps, a short time of adjustment. This, you will find, is a pleasant, energising and rejuvenating feeling. Be aware of these changes and enjoy them.

3. You will also find yourself interacting with others in ways which may surprise you. The truth may become extremely important to you, and you may find yourself saying things which rock the boat of your relationships. Should this happen, see it as a passing phase of acclimatisation to the rarity of the atmosphere around you. Later, you

will know how to express your truth in a more compassionate and less urgent way, which will cause fewer upsets. However, express your truth you will, for that is the vibration you will be on, and nothing less will fit you. Being true to yourself can become something of a burden, even though less of a burden than the results of its opposite. Do not let your truth burden you – wear and dispense it lightly. It is ultimately only your truth after all.

4. Then there is the issue of disparity. Sometimes you may well feel that life on your earth is so unfair, there must be no-one watching who cares. As you journey up the staircase and see further, that feeling may be heightened. Please remember that this disparity you see is part of the illusion of your making. There is no comparison possible, between peoples' destinies. It is all far too complex for that. Remember everyone is acting out his or her own play, and, as in any play, the roles vary widely. Because humans have free will, you have chosen a huge variety of roles to play, over many lifetimes of experience. What has been chosen is being played out. This is not to say those suffering would wish it so in this life they find themselves in. But, at a far more long-term level, these are the roles they have picked, for their own development. There are the individual reasons as well as the collective ones. Nothing goes unnoticed by those who care about you all, and help is constantly given to the players. So accept what you see, help where you can, and move on.

5. On your flight of stairs you may sometimes trip

a little, and find you have to retrace your steps. This is not a sign of failure, but of determination. When this happens, congratulate yourself for catching yourself before you fell further, and for getting up again. Enjoy the trip, as they say! Being judgemental towards yourself will only push you down a few more steps. Sometimes you will find, too, that you hit a plateau, and do not move on for a while. This is a needed time of adjustment and consolidation. The air may become too rarified for you if you did not stop and acclimatise once in a while. So be easy on yourself, and flow with whatever pattern of climb you need.

6. When you are little people, in your mothers' arms, most of you know what security feels like. You do not strive for anything else – you are content. But something happens at some point, so that by the time you are adults, most of you struggle to attain that same sense of security and stability. It seems to have deserted you, and you miss it. In your strivings to find it again, you try many things, inwardly and mostly outwardly, but in most cases, they are not fully satisfactory, and the search goes on. From the quality of this search, you glean that it is not easy to be a person here on earth, and that struggle is the normal state of affairs. This is a sad affair for us to witness, as we know it need not be so. It is also not a helpful attitude for climbing the staircase. You are all shielded all the time, by beings who love you, and are eager to help you. That sense of being in your mothers' arms would remain with you, if you could see into

the other realms surrounding you. There is, as we have said, never a time when you are alone. Once you can attune yourselves to the other densities around you, you will take great comfort from this. Whenever you are in a state of doubt about your support in the world, we suggest you ask for some evidence of it. Then look, listen and feel. You will be given signs that will confirm what we are telling you. Signs such as strange smells, feelings, tastes, words, happenings. Accept them as signals of another reality and not of impending insanity. We ask you to do this regularly, until you are accustomed to the notion of there being more than the three dimensional world around you. You will be forming stronger links with these other realms, by doing this, and it then becomes easier for these beings to help you. Once you are fully attuned to multiple realms, you will need no advice, because, at this point, you will have such clear guidance that you will know what to do, and will feel fully supported and secure. Until then, be open and be fluid to the signals which come your way. It will be easier to climb the staircase when you feel secure and connected.

7. Here is another simple technique for enlightenment of the soul. 'Simple!' you cry 'We thought enlightenment was a life-long pursuit!' It does not have to be. Enlightenment, merely means becoming lighter, freer of burdens, and more able to connect with the source central to your being. It does not have to be a burdensome struggle – enduring silence, fasting and freezing

in isolated mountainous terrain. No, there are far more pleasant ways to become enlightened, and ways which would suit your lifestyle far better. By resting upon your truth, you will find you become lighter. Lack of integrity forms a heavy burden, which must be carried wherever you go. You have a central core of values, ideas and beliefs – your interpretation of the way of the world, and your place in it. These ideas are neither right nor wrong. The important thing is that they reflect your learning thus far. Hopefully they will change with time, as you learn more. Each time you behave in a way which is congruent with this core, you are remaining free. Each time you behave in a way which crosses this core, you are forming a weight to carry in your backpack. It works like this: the vibrations of your energy system resonate to that core of thinking, values and so on. Each time you act in accordance with them, you resonate with who you already are, and there is no conflict. But when you act out of sync with this resonance, you create a counter current or vibration, which conflicts with the pre-existing one. This causes inner conflict, and slows down your progress. You have created a problem, which will later need to be reversed somehow. 'Well, what happens when you take on new information and act according to that?' you ask. This is different. You have your pre-existing resonance of ideas. New information interacting with an open mind merely slots in and changes this resonance to a slightly different one. When you act according to this new resonance, you are in sync and remaining free and unencumbered.

If, however, you resist new information, you can certainly set up a conflicting counter current, which eventually, will need addressing. Enlightenment can be facilitated by honouring your integrity constantly. If you do this, you will gradually reduce the backpack you may have been carrying, and find yourself heading to freedom and insight. This involves the development of certain skills and abilities. To honour your own integrity, you must be aware of who you are and what you stand for; you must be able to recognise your own feelings and thoughts so that you can express them appropriately; and you must be able to do these things in a manner which causes no-one around you harm. If you cause harm while you act in your own integrity, the ripples of the effect of your actions will come bouncing back to you, causing discord rather than enlightenment. Perhaps more often, the factor of fitting in with others takes first place, instead of equal place. So as not to lose affection or acceptance, so as not to hurt a fragile one's feelings, you deny your own truth, and cause yourself the inner discord you strove to avoid. This is a damaging pattern, which, over time, may lose you to yourself. You may find you become so focussed on the other's values, that you forget your own. You are then acting as a shadow of the other, rather than as the free person you were meant to be. Shadows are not enlightening! So be true to yourself, taking others into account. That is fairer to the others after all – then they know who they are dealing with. Your integrity will help you all up the staircase.

Peace through understanding

Until a state is reached wherein you are at peace with each other, there will be much conflict in your world. There is one lasting way to achieve peace ultimately, and this is through understanding that you are all one. Once you reach the top of the staircase, you will understand this. If you bear these tips in mind as you wend your way, you will find it a simpler and more direct route to the top.

Peace is what you all want. Before there is an understanding of the Oneness of all life, how to find peace? It is found through harmony. This may sound like a conundrum. But peace and harmony are not the same thing. Peace comes about as a result of harmony. And harmony comes about as a result of total commitment to it.

How to be committed to harmony? You have to start by being harmonious within yourself, before you will be harmonious with others. This entails loving yourself – all of yourself. Not just the 'good' bits. It entails accepting yourself as you are, not as you could be or should be. Of course, accepting yourself fully cannot be done properly unless you know yourself fully. Saying you accept what you do not know is merely a sham.

Self-acceptance is the basis of peace

So the first step in achieving peace in your world is probably to know yourself better. If you are able to remove the judgements about yourself that spring to mind instantly, you will be better able to have a good and unbiased look at yourself. It is not about judging, it is about knowing and accepting. This does not mean you might not want to change or adapt some of your patterns, habits or personality traits – that is fine. But in order to do this you must first see what is there and accept it is there. There is no point in fighting with yourself and pretending you are something you are not. This is a good basis for disharmony, within yourself, and among others. If you accept yourself at a deep level, others' judgements will not touch you. If you are able to accept yourself in this way, you will be more likely to accept others, and conflict will be less likely to occur.

Accepting yourself does not mean saying 'look what a silly person I am- that's just me.' It means appreciating yourself for who you are without judging at all. It means seeing and honouring the bits you find helpful and the bits you find unhelpful; the bits you are comfortable with and the bits you are not. Knowing that, as parts of you, they all have their place. You may also know that they are changeable. That is another step. But first they must be accepted as they are. Once you can do that, you are on the way towards peace. If you are always struggling to push into oblivion certain parts of you that you don't accept, and want no-one else to see, you are constantly at war. This war is bound to manifest on the outside, between you and others. If there are parts of you that you must hide from others, then you need to erect defences to keep others safely at bay, so they will not get too close and see your secrets. As soon as you walk around with defences you will attract attack. People will want to cross the barriers to see what juicy morsel you are hiding! In a trice your own defence has turned into counter attack, and the battle is on. The safer defence is to accept yourself in the first place. Then when others see you, there is no problem, and no battle to be waged.

Until then...

On your journey you will need much patience, with yourself and others. You may well find this patience does not come easily. The society you have been living in does not value patience. It values quick returns, and has little tolerance for deliberation or slowness. But patience does not equal tardiness. It is a sign of wisdom and requires, at times, much restraint. Again, your societies have generally forgotten the art of restraint. The common unspoken motto is: the more the merrier; the quicker the better; and me first at any cost. 'Go for it!' Someone who shows restraint is often interpreted as being weak, indecisive, or lacking in confidence. Nothing could be further from the truth. Restraint is an indication of independence, of confidence in your ability to wait or to manage without. It is a sign of strength. It often indicates a broader view point than the short-term personal one.

Patience and restraint

You will have many opportunities to practise patience and restraint, as these are qualities you will need to develop before you are ready to access your paradise.

In order to develop patience, you will give yourself

opportunities to experience its opposite. Situations will arise which push you to extreme impatience. You will be forced to consider restraint as an option, if you wish to become more patient. Impatience is an uncomfortable state, is it not? So you will lead yourself along towards a more comfortable way.

One of the key tricks to being patient is to be fully in the present. Impatience, after all, is about rushing into the next moment – about wanting something to happen which has not yet happened. So, if you divorce yourself from the future, and sit firmly in the present, there is no space for impatience. This way, you do not even need restraint. You are simply being. This way you can enjoy the richness of the moment, without missing out on anything.

Non-judgement reduces impatience

You will also find that an absence of judgement helps in reducing impatience with others. If you judge each person to be perfect just the way they are, you cannot feel impatient when they are not a certain way. The same applies to yourself. If you accept yourself as you are, here and now, there will be no impatience with yourself, as there will not be perceived shortcomings. This does not mean being stuck and unable to grow or move on. It merely implies that within the journey you are on, you know you are doing your best. This is always true, no matter how it may seem.

CHAPTER 19

Rolling with the Times

We have spoken often about time and about change – both aspects of your current world. Although mankind has always lived with these, he has not effectively mastered either of them. Instead he looks at ways of overcoming them through controlling or resisting them as best he can. This is exhausting and always proves futile.

Your most common way of dealing with time is to divide it into small chunks – the same reductionist method your scientists employ. You believe time will be manageable if you can slice it up and control the contents of the slices. But in so doing you are losing time altogether. This is because time is not divisible, and in dividing it up it is destroyed. The only real way to manage time is to be in it, and thus to be part of it. In this way none of it is lost, and everything is fully experienced. You do not understand? Let us put it this way: as soon as you divide up time into past present and future, you lose the present, which is really all you ever have. Every time you invest in the past or future, you diminish the present.

Thought versus experience

It is only when you are fully present that you can experience. The rest of the time you are merely thinking, as the future and past only exist in your mind. If you humans have chosen to be here to experience life, why would you want to waste most of it on thinking instead? Staying in the present has become something of an art for you, instead of the natural way of being, which it was originally. If you cultivate the habit of being present, life becomes so much richer, and you can evolve more easily into who you are. This is because when you are present you are with yourself, not elsewhere. Thus are you able to hear the cues that lead you on into your life. When you are in the past or future, you are, in effect, denying life, and thereby stultifying your own evolution.

Timelessness

When you are fully conscious there is no time, because, you could say, everything is time. So time, not being separately definable, ceases to exist. This is how you will experience time eventually. This is what is known as the end of time. Until then, try to take time less seriously than you used to. See it as the background for your present, rather than a ruling deity! Manage it according to how you feel intuitively, rather than letting it manage you. Let it slip into the background of a continuous present. That way you will be building stepping stones to where you are headed.

Inevitable change

Then the issue of managing change: for most of you change is seen as an undesirable break in your routine, at best, and as a severe threat to your well-being or safety at worst. When you are thinking in this way you are completely missing the greater picture of your life.

Now you might have forgotten, but you did not come into this life to find a comfy niche of some sort, and stay there. You came to experience, to experiment and to grow and evolve into who you are. Therefore change is an inevitable part of the plan you set in place for your life. One way or another, your soul will ensure that changes come your way, to give you the opportunity of responding to them and thus growing. If you resist change in one form, it will be thrown at you in another. So, if, for instance, you stay entrenched in the same job or relationship long after you lose interest in it, you may become ill. The symptoms of your illness introduce some elements of change into your life, giving you some opportunity for response and growth. You may have understood this turn of events to mean 'the boring job made me sick', but it is more complex than merely that. In denying yourself the opportunity of growth by changing jobs or relationships, you are forcing another change upon yourself, for, whatever the cost, change you must have.

Contrast and cycles

This is one of the reasons so many people who ride the crest of the financial wave for too long find themselves suddenly bankrupt one day. They have taken what they can from that experience, and now need some contrast to respond to. And this is one of the reasons your world and all in it is based on cycles. Light gives way to dark; high tide to low tide; life to death; happiness to pain. Thus must it be until you have experienced all you need to experience to remember who you are. Once you are all aware of who you really are, these cycles will no longer be necessary, although you might choose to create them anyway, for interest.

Writing the script of life

So look upon the changes which come your way as gifts and opportunities for remembrance and growth, not as challenges or threats. Remember too that in responding to them there is no right answer which you are obliged to find. There is no-one up there who will smack you on the wrist if you get it wrong. You write the script as you go along. The first sentence of the script will have some bearing on the second. That is how you write the play of your life. There is no secret template of perfection which you must agonisingly seek. Everything you do is perfect. You are already perfect. It is not about being perfect. It is about experiencing. And what better way to experience than to accept change, and roll with it. Adopt a 'let's see what happens now' approach, as you move into the next phase of your life. Many of you tend to create difficulties for yourselves by adopting a 'what do I have to do to stop this happening?' approach. The effect of this is like putting on the brakes when you're already in a skid. It causes accidents and injuries. Now there is nothing wrong with accidents and injuries, but we believe most of you would not consciously choose them, as you value happiness and do not equate them with that.

Consciously riding into change

So before you resist change, step back, take a look at the larger picture of your life, and, if the change seems to fit into this larger context, go for it without looking back. Ride into change on the horse of timelessness. Change is much easier if you do not spend energy on worries about the future, or comparisons with the past. Just attend to the present, and you will find it is not only manageable, but may even be joyful.

Of course we are not suggesting moving blindly into silly situations. You need to be conscious in choosing which branches of change to grow and which to prune. You will continue to have free will, and must exercise it with discrimination and awareness. Awareness is not the same as worry or distraction. Awareness here means being open-eyed, both to your own heart and intuition, and to the probable consequences of your choices. It does not refer to awareness of what others or society would prefer you to do. On this journey, which is yours alone, that is hardly relevant. Remember, your journey might take you in ways which oppose the mainstream of society. Remember too that the mainstream of society, as it is now will be relatively short-lived. It is in a state of flux and will be changing radically. So if you let that dictate your decisions, you may be left behind. Now is the time to go by your own soul.

Change does not come only to those who seek it. It comes to you all. If you actively seek it out, you may find you have more conscious control over how it affects your life. If you just do nothing and wait to be swept along, this is exactly what will happen. No way is better. It is up to you to choose.

Dealing with pressure

There may be times when you feel pressured into doing or saying something. This pressure may come from within or without. Just because it comes from within does not mean it is helpful. Pressure is never a good basis for creativity. It suggests a force rather than an unfolding. As we have mentioned, many influences are being exerted upon all of you these days, some more benevolent than others. The messages of the benevolent ones are not usually experienced as pressure. Rather they are quiet, like your intuition, and respectful of your own free will and activities. So any pressured message heard internally is probably not from a benevolent source. This source may, of course, merely be a part of your own consciousness.

Then there is pressure from external sources – family, friends, society. If this pressure is asking you to follow routes you have already decided to follow, that is fine. But if it is asking you to diverge from your chosen path, ignore it. No-one knows your way better than you. Pressure usually indicates a need on the part of the person pressing. This need does not necessarily fit with yours, and you do not necessarily have to fulfil it.

So be alert to pressure and what it means. Be alert too, to your response to it. Sometimes people can block their own chosen path through refusing to bow to pressure on principle. This is unwise. You may find you are pressured to join certain groups or movements, or ways of thinking. Be very careful that you do not allow others to pull you away from your own integrity, for the sake of acceptance. It is never worth it in the long run. You do not need to make a stand in order to quietly follow your own way.

CHAPTER 20

The Truth of the Matter

Dear friends, you have succeeded in accomplishing so many amazing things in your playground, but most of you have not yet worked out what it is made of! Matter is not what it seems. The chair you are sitting on is not as solid as it seems to you. You could go through it if you wanted to. Your scientists are fascinated because it seems to them that if they condensed all the matter of the earth, it would fit onto a pinhead. This is not so. This is because scientists, clever though they are, can only hypothesise about what they already know. Because in the past they have not been able to see energy under a microscope, they have not taken it into their equations. However, at last, they are finding out it actually exists. Not only that, it holds your whole world together. Take it away, and there would literally only be inert fragments.

The hum of life

So the chair upon which you sit is alive. It is moving, it is feeling, it is, in a sense, breathing, in that it is constantly exchanging energy with its environment. Everything around you, in your home, in your garden, in your work place, is alive. There is no dead piece of cardboard or sleeping rock. Everything hums. And that hum affects you, the humans in the midst of it. This is profoundly important to you. The quality of the hum or vibration dictates your own, to a large extent, because it is in constant exchange with you. Remember, there are no boundaries in reality – everything is linked. This link is not just slight as in the linear links of a chain. It is complete, as in a hologram. Until you learn to create your own frequency, independent of your environment, you will be an interdependent part of the hologram.

You are able to learn to create your own tune, because of your unique potential. If you identify more strongly with this infinite potential than with the material world, you will be more able to override the surrounding vibratory effect. You will then be able to transmit your own frequency into the world, without being affected by it. This is a position of great power.

Finding the empty lane

This is not science fiction, it is the fact of the matter, so to speak. It is all common sense. Just because you have not been able to see it, does not mean it is not happening. Liken it to driving in traffic. When you are in the same lane as everyone else at rush hour, you crawl along at everyone else's pace. However, if you cross into an empty lane, suddenly you are free to go at your own pace. This is exactly how it works. The trick in your world is in finding that empty lane. We will discuss some ways in which you can access it:

1. Firstly, you have all heard of meditation. This is indeed one of the best ways to access the empty

lane. It allows for a loosening of ties to the everyday outside world, and a strengthening of ties to the inner reality.

2. Then there is just being, which we have discussed. Doing strengthens your ties to the outer world, being to the inner world. When you are connecting to the inner world, you may be attending to your emotions, thoughts or dreams, or transcending these to the level beyond, which is pure consciousness. You will be able to tell the difference, as the only one of these states to bring peace is the latter.

3. One of the ways of becoming aware of your real nature is through the natural world. When you enjoy a sunset or a flower, a waterfall or the sea, you are opening yourself to the energy of creation. The vibration of creation passes through you, which is one of the reasons these experiences are so enjoyable. It reminds you of who you really are, and temporarily separates you from the densities around you, which diminish you.

4. Another way is through art. This, too, may be an expression of pure consciousness, or it may be inspired by various aspects of the personality. The creative process itself may open a channel to your higher dimensions, and the viewing of art may inspire a similar opening.

Whichever way you choose does not matter. There is no better or worse way. It just depends on what suits you, for you are all different, with different histories and different preferences. Whether or not you meditate, whether or not you paint or go to forests, ultimately, if you want to find the way to connect, you will. It all comes back to your intent. The will finds a way.

Investing in the eternal

So we would ask you, where is all your drive? Where is all your passion? Is it not time you retrieved it from the supermarket and phones, from the television and sports fields, from the Financial Times and the share market? If some of the energy you invest in these transitory pursuits were rather invested in your future, it would be a good thing for all. You ask what we mean by transitory pursuits – it seems to you these are what life is made of. Yes, friends, once it was, but it will not be for long. The world you are travelling towards is a very different world, strange as it may seem. We are not talking about centuries away - we are talking about soon. It sounds impossible to you that the world – the only one you know, could soon be so altered. But the impossible happens every day. What you call 'miracles' are only so named because you do not understand their workings. They are no more strange than anything else. They are just not understood. What you understand in your world, you have clasped to you, relying upon it to serve your every need. The misunderstood elements of your world you have pushed away, so that you can relish a sense of undisturbed certainty. However, the comfort of these times has come to an end. You are being faced with so many inconsistencies now, that to continue to only see what you understand, you would have to be blind. This will undoubtedly be the choice of some people. We hope it will not be yours, as there will be so much beauty in your future, it would be a pity to miss it.

Allowing uncertainty

While you await the changes, you will pass through many phases of being. There will be times when you are in despair, times of great elation, times of hope, times of grief. These are already mapped out in your probable future, as they are needed to shift you to the possibility of entering the world that awaits you. While you are tied to the current world, you will not be able to enter the new one. You cannot take your dog for a walk while he is tied by his lead to the fence, can you? First you need to untie him. It is just the same with you, friends. You cannot possibly know what joy and elation await you, but you cannot get there unless you release your hold on your current realities. There are easier and more difficult ways to do this. If your dog is frightened of going to the park for a walk, he might cower against the fence, and not allow you to undo his lead. In that case, you might have to pull him away from the fence, or perhaps pick him up and carry him away. He might feel his trust in you has been violated. When he gets to the park, it would all be worth it, but he might go through some angst on the way.

You are all the dogs on the lead of your current reality. If you choose to go to the park willingly, knowing what may lie ahead, and preparing for this, it will be so much more pleasant for you, than if you choose to be out of step with your destiny, and resist. So, untie yourselves now – start getting used to the freedom you have within you, for you will carry that wherever you go.

Chasing freedom

How to do this?

- Start to question.
- Question the validity of some of your assumptions.
- Question the validity of your use of time, of your current values.
- Question the way you judge things and people.
- Question your language.
- Question the usefulness and integrity of your society, its structures and mores.
- Question your expectations.
- Push yourself to look beyond where you would normally go.
- See the other side of situations.
- Try what you have never tried before.
- Surprise yourself.
- Stare into your shadow.
- Notice how others reflect you.
- See the nuances, and not just the black and white.
- Believe there is more to be found, more to be seen, more to be understood. Seek it out, however you can.

- Be open to ideas that may shock you. Take shock as a sign of possible growth.

- Look for evidence.

- Explore most deeply what you feel most certain about – that is often what ties you to the fence.

- Spend more time on your senses – listen, smell, feel, taste, touch. This is the way to dispel nonsense! Your senses, ultimately, can lead you to the truth. They exist only here and now, and that is, after all, where truth and power reside.

- Notice all the messages your body gives you. They are all clues to who you are, what you think and what you feel.

- Get to know yourself – who you really are, not what roles you play, or how you may appear to others.

Dancing a new destiny

As you loosen your grip on the old certainties, you will be creating for yourself a new reality, which is more flexible and more likely to be compatible with the future.

Allow yourself to resonate with like-minded souls. This is very helpful on what may seem a lonely journey at times. Maintain the thread of the joy of becoming. In every moment, whatever you are doing, you are becoming a new person. Is this not an exciting creation you are embarked upon? So do not be too heavy about it all, or you will be defeating part of the purpose, which is about moving into light. There is no point in shining a light upon yourself and your world, if you then throw upon it a shadow of serious conscientiousness. Play your way into understanding.

Dance your way into your destiny. That way, the light you gain will remain shining brightly, undimmed by duty, which is not a happy concept. You were born to be happy beings – beings of light. When shadows are thrown at you, do not darken them for too long with grief. Instead, seek out the patches of light you can find, to support you in your return to your natural state.

A bird's eye view

There is much in your current world that is of concern to you. Do not give it too much heed. Focus on seeing beyond the obvious, as circumstances are not always what they seems to be. Float slightly above and beyond what is happening around you. This does not mean 'do not feel', 'be vague' or 'ignore issues and events'. It merely means that you need to put a little distance between yourself and the events of your world, so that you can see them, and the road ahead, more clearly. If the world cries out for vengeance, step back and notice what you see and hear. If panic blocks the sun of your days, take a deep breath, go outside, sit down and let your mind move away from it. From another place, you will know what you need to do. Do not get caught up in the collective frenzy. Only when the collective response creates a happy feeling in you, is it wise to join them. In all other cases, step back and assess quietly for yourself.

Your unique path

The time is coming when you will need to be independent in this way. You will need to be able to think for yourself and know what you feel most certain about. Many will make different choices from yours, and to go along with the crowd's response will be to dishonour your own direction. The majority is not 'always right'. Only you know what is right for you, for each of you is on a unique path. Do not allow others, who may not have your courage or vision, to change your direction. Use the energy of their opposition as fuel for your journey.

Once you have found out who you are and where you are headed, you will no longer need this advice. But until then, be sure that you spend long hours looking in the mirror of your reality, to become acquainted intimately with your own nature. If your reality is showing you things you do not like – seek these within yourself, and seek to change them. If your world is presenting you with wonderful beauty and happiness, appreciate that this is what you are. If you find yourself in conflict, go within and make peace between the conflicting elements of yourself. Internal balance reaps external balance, which is more needed now in your world, than ever before.

Savouring the road to glory

To deny yourself the beauty of your journey by focussing on the hard parts, would be to waste a golden opportunity. Your collective journey into the future as a species, will be noteworthy, to say the least. It will be the culmination of aeons of experience and experiment. It will be the crowning glory of all your achievements and the grand finale of your symphony. You might as well watch the passing parade, don't you think? So see everything that happens from here on as part of a glorious progress of evolution. Please do not see it as a trial, disintegration, or threat. When a child fails an exam, he is still part of the school system, working his way up to being a well-educated adult. You, too, may have disruptions, but they will only be part of the road ahead to glory.

There is also the matter of fruition. All things come to fruition in their own time. There is no speeding up the opening of a flower, the ripening of a peach, or the meeting with opportunity. It must happen in its own time. Hence we say to you, do not be impatient. The amount of time which will pass before you arrive at your destination will depend on many factors, most of which you will be unable to control. So stay in the present, enjoy every moment available to you, and do not count the minutes to your destiny.

CHAPTER 21

Past Times

Back in the 'old days' when people had fewer choices, it was not so difficult to make a decision. There was white bread or brown bread. However now you may find yourselves mentally running around in ever-decreasing circles when you are confronted with the daily dose of decision-making. It threatens to swamp many of you, and lower your vitality.

'There must be a way round this' you tell yourselves, vainly trying new goal-setting methods, time-management diaries, personal coaches and priority lists. But these are not the answer to your dilemma. They only give you more cause for decision-making. What is more important – attending that workshop on change management, or taking your daughter to the kindergarten fete? So let us look at an alternate way of managing this crisis of busy-ness.

Wisdom in stillness

The way most of you have not considered is the way of stillness. We know we have mentioned this before, but it bears mentioning again and again. When you are still, an extraordinary thing happens. You start to connect with yourself. In connecting with yourself, you are able to access your wisdom. It is from this place that good decisions are made. Too often, in your societies, decisions are made based on monetary considerations above all. But what is money? It is only a conduit, through which exchange of energy flows. If you feed the conduit itself, eventually it becomes so bloated that nothing can flow through it. So not money, but direction, should be your priority. If your decisions are taking you in appropriate and sustainable directions, the money will flow as a by-product.

Decision-making and the impotent past

In order to master the art of decision-making, you will need to be in the present and understand the place of the past.

The past is like an old cloth – tatty and holed, flimsy and faded, yet still bearing shreds of colour. It is the long-forgotten and the outmoded; the backstage of your today and the shadow behind your tomorrow.

But the past, in reality, has no power of itself. If anything, more often than not, it shuts off access to power. This is only the case when you give the past permission to overtake the present, or define the limits wherein the present may operate. Remember, the past is gone, and has already been acted out. The players have left the stage and the curtain has been closed. It is up to you whether or not you leave that curtain closed, or whether you keep peeking; whether you let those players go home and to bed, or keep pulling them back onto your stage. Your psychologists would have it that your past is very defining for you

– this has become a strong myth of your times. And, indeed, it would seem to many of you that you can only build upon what you were yesterday. Well, we have news for you! Yes, that was true for much of your history, but it is no longer so.

Reinventing reality

So much has changed in your world in recent times that your today need bear little resemblance to your yesterday, if you so choose. We keep stressing the power you have, as this is still not fully understood. You can reinvent reality for yourself on a daily basis. You are now able to access abilities, knowledge, identity for which you have had no training in the past. You are able to change conditions, habits, thinking and feeling patterns at will. The energy field around you now supports jumps in consciousness as never before. You can switch yourself from whoa to go in an instant if you so wish.

How does this work? Quite simply, rather as a light switch does. The switch is off and no light shines. You decide you want light, move the switch to 'on', and the light shines forth. The mechanism may be mysterious and hidden, known only to a few electricians, physicists and so on, who probably don't fully understand it either. But, in order for you to achieve light, you don't need to understand all the workings behind the scenes. All you need is the desire for it, and a simple action, and abracadabra, it is done! That is the best way for you to understand much of your world, for there is so much depth and mystery, so much paradox and possibility that, were you to try to unravel all the secrets you would have no time left to live and enjoy them. You would also wear yourself out, as there are no answers for many of the questions you would be asking. Accept mystery rather than trying to dissect it, then you can start living to the full within it.

Feeding the present to the past

The past, too, is a mystery – one which you could spend years trying to unravel and decode. But the present moments which are used up on such a quest are usually more valuable than the knowledge eventually gained through such analysis. It is as though you are feeding your present to your past, when you engage in such pursuits now. A little understanding, yes, but great analysis and soul searching regarding the past is now counterproductive. This time you are in is so different that there can be no comparison made. What happened then does not need to bear any relationship to what happens now, so why bother?

The past is a shadow which lurks behind, ready to trip up and catch the unwary in its grip. Focus instead on where you are and where you seek to be. That is where your power and your assistance lie.

Setting your compass in magic times

Once you know where you are and where you want to head to, you are at least halfway there. Sometimes you will find you are in fact already there. Sometimes the intent is all it takes. In other cases some external affirmation in the form of action is needed, to bring your destination into reality. There are many cases in which people have suffered through rigorous training schedules to fulfil criteria or demands which they believe will lead them closer to the goal. Generally, now, if you find yourself following this sort of pattern, we suggest that either your goal is inappropriate, or your method of reaching it is ineffective. This is because you are now living in a time of magic. If you are still stumbling along when you can fly, then you are using an outdated mode of transport.

Stop for a moment and think of all the odd things which have happened to you in the past few years. The synchronicities, the dreams, the insights, the miracles, the prophesies, the visions, the sudden changes to your life. These are happening more and more to everyone now, and they did not used to happen like this. Mankind was operating at a denser level, and was slower in every way, more bound to the concrete and less empowered to shift his reality exponentially. In those days there was a plodding, a pottering through the material world of man's reality, with only the blessed few glimpsing eternity. Please believe us, this has changed completely. Now, if something miraculous doesn't happen to most of you at least once a year, we would be surprised. The veil between you and reality is becoming thinner, and you are catching glimpses regularly. Let these glimpses be your guide to where you are headed. Let the past go and become the relic it is.

CHAPTER 22

Jump Down, Turn Round

It is time to be frisky, time to make hay and time to celebrate. Why? Because this is the only time you have, and you may as well make the most of it. We believe you to be very lucky to be there on Planet Earth. It is one of the best playgrounds to be found anywhere. Yet, we are surprised to see so few of you actually enjoying yourselves. You are immersed in unnecessary struggle, rather than delightful play. You are focussing on the problems rather than the beauty. Of course there are both, but why give your energy to the less pleasant one? While you are here, you might as well enjoy yourselves.

Lightness of being

There is no virtue in struggle, and no great merit in seriousness. It was never decreed that the human should at all times be sensible and work hard. You are here to be experiencers. So why not experience lightness of being, rather than heaviness? When you are light it is easier to leap to all sorts of places you cannot access if you are plodding, bound to the earth by seriousness and earnest intent.

We are not advocating frivolousness to the extent

of denial of care or sensitivity. We are merely inviting you to take advantage of your glorious opportunities to have fun. There are places to be explored, activities to be tried, people to be met, colours to be felt and tastes to be seen. So why is it you tend to repeat the same experiences over and over again, with so little enthusiasm? Opportunities for enjoyment and delight face you each day in your lives, yet many of you usually turn away to the mundane, the already known. Perhaps you set aside Friday night for fun, while the rest of the week is duty and chores. We see this as odd.

Counting happiness

We have some ideas about what is happening here, which we will share with you.

Because most of you are so tied to your material world and its benefits, you are forgetting the benefit of the immaterial, the invisible. Emotions are immaterial and joy is invisible. Because you cannot count or see these, you are undervaluing them. How often do your politicians stand on a platform of happiness for their electorate? Never! Instead they measure their electorates possible happiness in terms of employment, lower taxes, health-care systems and other such scenarios. All of these can be counted and many statistics are quoted to back up the claims of various would-be power players. But you cannot put happiness, fun, joy or laughter into statistics. Imagine it: 'If I get elected I promise you that each one of my electorate in Lower Watherington will have cause to laugh at least twice daily.' It doesn't and cannot happen. So the values of your societies have come to be clearly defined as ones which can be counted. How much you earn, how big your house is, what suburb you can afford to live in, how many degrees you have, how big your antique collection is, how much your insurance covers you for. There is nothing in there about beauty or happiness. They don't count, literally. And what doesn't count becomes devalued in your societies.

A different stock-take

Now, most of you, if you stopped to think about it at all, would see yourselves as small cogs in the wheel of society, playing your part, and, more importantly, surviving. While you survive, you also try to score what 'goodies' as you can from society. How do you measure which 'goodies' are worth going for? Over time you have come to accept that what is seen and spoken of the most is worth the most. So those with fewer goods, jobs, and dollars are seen to be 'worse off.' This may not be the case at all. There are many people with all the 'goodies', who are absolutely lacking in joy, who seldom laugh and who have forgotten what fun really is. And many who have little visible wealth but know how to be happy.

So the human race has collectively undervalued fun itself. Instead all the pursuits which lead to the accumulation of material wealth have been over-emphasised. So many of you work long hours, take second jobs to pay large mortgages, keep busy at weekends looking after your possessions, and collapse in front of the TV in between, as a way of resting.

Where is the joy in all this?

Imagine if each laugh was worth $20, if each moment of happiness was worth $30, each experience of joy $40, each thrill from a new experience $50, each delight in something beautiful $35, each fascinating discovery $50 and each moment of fun $40! How your society's values would change over night! Suddenly people would be competing to have fun; would be queueing to be delighted; would be falling over each other to try new experiences. Aaah well... one can dream!

Appreciating joy

In reality, the values of these experiences are far greater than any numerical value which could be attributed to them. They are so close to what life is made of – love – that they are actually supportive of life itself. Of course some material possessions can yield moments of joy, but these are usually rather fleeting, and soon the material possession becomes taken for granted and the joy is faded. Whereas, if you can learn to find joy and delight wherever you are, in the small moments, in the tiny discoveries, you have a life-long treasure. This is not difficult to do. It involves two main attributes: appreciation and perceptiveness. You may see many beautiful things around you, but unless you appreciate them, and the gift they bring, you will not translate this into happiness. On the other hand, you may be an appreciative person, but if you do not slow down enough to smell the roses or listen to the joke, you may be missing out on many possible objects of your appreciation, and causes for your smile.

Dancing through life

So be on the lookout for possible stimulants of happiness. They abound. Notice them, respond to them, then dance on to the next ones. Life does not have to be a drag. Rather, it is meant to be a twirl! You will probably find, if you access the twirl in your life, that you actually accomplish more, not less, because you are more energised, more focussed and more flexible. Have patience with those still plodding–they might not yet have heard of the possibility of twirling! Give them time. They may well notice your style and like it, after minor grumbles and objections.

It is lightness which will carry your world forward to its destination. It is heaviness which will hold it back. By having fun, you are actually helping your world! So next time you decide on another evening in front of the TV, or afternoon trudging around the shopping centre, remind yourself of all those things you could do, which would give you a buzz, lift your spirits or cause you to laugh out loud. All the things you meant to do 'one day' for fun are still waiting for you, and this is 'one day.' Enjoy your life – it is magic.

CHAPTER 23

The Merry-go-round

You are living your lives based upon sets of assumptions. These play a large part in your decision-making, therefore it would be empowering for you to know what they are.

Just as you each come into your life with a set of past experiences, and develop unique ways of being and of interacting with the world, you each carry your own unique combinations of assumptions about life and the world. However, there are some assumptions that we see virtually the whole of the human race carrying, and these are having a strong influence on the direction in which you steer your world.

Let us examine some of these.

Assumptions about liberty

Firstly the assumptions about liberty. Humans seem to assume that freedom is a state which they can grant each other, or of which they can deprive each other. This is not, and has never been the case. Liberty pre-exists human will. Liberty is a given condition of all human beings. It is the conditions in which humans sometimes find themselves, which have led them to believe it is a variable state. These conditions may include incarceration, deprivation, domination, even torture. Terrible though these may seem, within each of these circumstances, the individual's liberty is never at question. The young mother, who is woken in the night and virtually enslaved by her baby's needs for years, does not regard herself as being deprived of her liberty, yet the prisoner of war does. What is the difference? The young mother might have chosen her situation, unlike the prisoner, however in both cases, the individual's range of actions is curtailed by the circumstances and their demands. Yet the liberty of these individuals remains. What, then, is liberty? It is the freedom to respond to a given set of circumstances, and the freedom to initiate or create something new within these situations. The response or creation may not be outwardly expressed – it may merely be a thought, an understanding, an idea, or, it may manifest as an outward action or speech. This interpretation of liberty is a prime reason some survive difficult times, while others succumb.

Much of the human race sees liberty in black or white terms. Either you have it, or you don't. From our viewpoint, it is not like this at all. In fact, in some of the countries which proclaim the greatest respect for human liberties, these liberties are being exercised the least by individuals, due to conformity to subtle but strong pressures such as economics, fashion, competitiveness, peer pressure, political correctness, and fear. And in some other countries, which, to the outsider, look very oppressive, the human soul is exercising its liberty in a wonderful, individual, if private, way. So the regime does not make the quality of liberty. It is how you play the game within the regime, which determines how much you are respecting your own liberty. You can have total permission and access, yet feel trapped; or you can be totally trapped, yet feel free.

Honouring your liberty

Understanding and honouring your own liberty – your birthright of free will – has always been important. It is now more important than ever.

You ask 'What is the point of free will in a situation wherein you have few choices – such as the slave or the prisoner?' There may be little you can physically do in these situations, but remember, you are only a partially physical being. Predominantly you are energetic – made of energy. This energy is affected by your thoughts, emotions, and will, and this energy, in turn, affects your body, and its health and abilities. So the prisoner may not have freedom of movement and may not be able to see the blue of the sky or eat what he fancies; but he still has freedom of thought, emotion and will. No-one can ever take that away from any other human being, without his collusion. Yet, this is usually what happens. The person in dire straits colludes with those circumstances and gives up his right to free will. When this occurs, he is unable to mentally or emotionally separate himself from his situation, and thus feels impelled to react classically instead of originally. In other words, if someone beats him, he feels fear and pain. If someone orders him, he feels submissiveness. This happens when a person forgets he is a separate entity from the event, and has the choice of inner response.

'But, ' you say, 'How could you feel anything but pain if you are being beaten – we're only human, after all.' Well, we would start by asking you to remove the 'only' from that sentence. Humans have a great capacity for ingenuity, for adaptiveness, for courage, for imagination and for distraction. A story has long done the rounds about a person with cancer, who, when asked by his friends if he was depressed about it, answered, 'No, it's bad enough having cancer. I wouldn't want to be depressed as well!' You always do have a choice about what you focus on. Admittedly, the more acute a situation is, the more difficult it might be to find free thought about it.

We have used the examples of slavery and imprisonment, not because we believe you will face these, but because you associate these with deprivation of liberty. However, in your daily lives, there are countless small instances in which you also take it for granted that you have no choice. There are few men who would dare to contemplate wearing a dress in your western societies, so strict is the unwritten code of conformity. You are at liberty to address the people on the train, even if everyone else's eyes are glazed over with privacy. Someone's anger towards you may prompt your return anger, your tolerance, your forgiveness, your humour, your silence, your bunch of flowers. The choice is yours, because you have free will.

If you honour your free will, rather than your conditioning, you will be more flexible and more adaptable to change. You may also be healthier, as you will probably not internalise as many emotions, unless, of course, you choose to.

Assumptions about words

The next set of assumptions we will explore revolves around credence.

People tend to assume that what has been put into words must necessarily be true. We would say that in perhaps 20% of cases this is so. The rest of the time, words mislead. Do not place too much credence on the words of your brothers and sisters. Read behind, above, below and between the words, to search for more accurate meaning. Words are often used as a political tool to gain advantage, rather than as a way of genuine information sharing. Words abound in your world. You see them on the internet, social media, emails, on billboards, magazines and newspapers. You hear them from television, movies, radio, phones and people around you. You are bombarded by them. How much of this do you swallow unquestioningly, inwardly digesting without a backward glance? We suggest far too much. Words are affecting your liberty. Many of you are actually being unwittingly brainwashed by the words of your societies. You are believing them rather than your own self, and thus depriving yourself of liberty – of the liberty of response or action chosen from a considered position.

The source of words

Think, for a moment about where many of the words of your society originate. Advertisers would have you buy their products, political parties would have you vote for them, the media would have you buy their papers or tune into their stations or pet beliefs, friends would have you see their point of view, writers would have you understand their ideas, magazine editors would have you conform to their images, so you will continue to buy their magazine and subsidize their advertisers. It seems there is usually a profit-oriented motive, one way or another. This most of you innocently disregard, as you go about your daily business of swallowing great word-meals whole. In a sense you are selling your souls to others' words, when you do this. In the absence of a regular stillness in which to tune into your own soul, you are allowing yourself to be dictated to by the collective, whose motives may stray far from your own.

So, if you want to retain your power, clarity and freedom of choice, learn to discriminate words more carefully. Look through them to their source and its needs, and decide whether you really want to fulfil these needs, or whether you, in fact, have other more important business to attend to.

We see most of you giving much credence too, to misguided words spoken by others in your personal relationships. Words may spring from emotions that are based upon illusory thought, and may be quite devoid of a realistic basis. They may be shot as punishment arrows by damaged egos, or thrust out as tentacles that entrap, by the needy. See past the words, to their motivations, their basis in truth, and your choices of response. In difficult times, particularly, you need to do what you can to retain your clarity, rather than responding blindly to the lack of it in others. This way you will not be assisting others in unhelpful machinations of the mind; you will not be manipulated; and will remain in touch with who you are and where you are going. Use words wisely, to share valid information.

Assumptions about beliefs

The next area of assumption that most of you stumble upon is that of belief. If only there were no such thing in your world, there would be so much more peace. What are beliefs apart from assumptions made after the gleaning of a few relevant bits of information, hopefully assumed to be 'facts'? Yet many of you seem to assume that a belief is a sacred item, to be revered and defended even at the cost of human life! 'I believe this, therefore it must be so, and you should believe it too, and if you don't you are a threat to me.' So people fight people and nations fight nations, in the name of religious beliefs, political beliefs, racial beliefs, historical beliefs. A belief is only a mind-set after all. It is changeable, or should be, with the advent of new information. Coming from so many different worlds, times, and lives, of course you would have formed different mind-sets. It is not rational to expect otherwise. The only rational response to the differences would be mutual respect.

Beliefs versus knowledge

A belief is not the same as knowledge. Knowledge comes from a different place, and is so secure it needs no defending. So, may we suggest that you learn to leave others to enjoy their beliefs in peace. Theirs are as valid as yours are. When, one day, more information has been gleaned, and the beliefs transmute into knowledge, it will be easier. But until then, allow each other to be. There is room on the earth for a huge range of beliefs, if you all respect each other. Start in your families. There is no reason the children should share the beliefs of the parents, and vice versa. Beliefs are things you discover for yourselves – no-one can foist them upon another. When this is the case, it is called domination, not belief.

And remember, your own beliefs need not be set in concrete, because beliefs, by nature, are pliable. Allow your beliefs access to new information which will shape them towards knowledge.

If you can bypass the common assumptions about liberty, credence and beliefs, you will be stepping off the human merry-go-round, and on to more solid ground. From here you are less likely to become dizzy and disorientated.

CHAPTER 24

Catering to Change

As you journey along on your life's path, you will have many crossroads, and will need to know how to deal with these. Some ways of handling crossroads are more effective than others, yet this, like so many important issues, is not a topic taught in your schools or universities. So we now offer you the missing lecture: Models for Moving into your Future.

Decision-making styles

Before you decide where you will go on holiday, you look up various destinations, price the options, discuss others' experiences, check availability and recall memories of past holidays you have enjoyed. Moving forward in time is a bit like this. As you venture into your future, many of you tend to refer to the past and to obvious current possibilities, to seek others' opinions, and to count possible costs. It can be a time-consuming process indeed. By the time you have decided which direction to step towards with your right foot, the options may have changed. This is, what we call, the 'deliberate method' of moving into your future. It is thought to be safer by its practitioners. 'It may be slow, but it's safe, because it's all well-planned', they think. Well, we agree to a point. It is slow, but it is not safe. Why is it not safe? Because it is cutting out so many options which would make it safer. The 'deliberate' practitioner is kept very busy mentally. According to his method, there is much thinking to be done before a decision is reached. He must consider all options carefully, weigh up, imagine consequences, take others into account, and so on. Now, we know these all sound very sensible things to be considering, especially before any major decision. But, the problem is, that the thinking involved actually limits the potential outcome of the decision-making process. Let us examine a specific case.

Limited and logical

Mr and Mrs Blarney want to buy a new house. They have been to the bank to ascertain how much they can borrow; they have looked at many house plans and have an idea of what they like; they have driven around various neighbourhoods to see which they would enjoy and could afford; and they have told several agents what they are looking for. The agent shows them 3 houses, each of which, if they are lucky, fits within their chosen criteria. Each of the criteria Mr and Mrs Blarney have set is based on the limitations of their thought processes. They are thereby cutting out all sorts of possibly exciting options. Yes, it seems sensible, but it is contained into a small box of logic, and cannot stretch to the magical.

Trusting and intuitive

Let us look at another way of moving forward. Mr

and Mrs Lark trust that there are forces in their world looking after them, and that, if they remain open, they can be led the best way. So, they set off innocently, a little vague about what they want, but clear on the general idea, and the core issues. They follow clues; they listen to their dreams; they watch the signs of the birds in the sky; they follow wild ideas; they notice their hearts beat; and they are led to the perfect house – one much better than they could possibly have imagined. This house has been found not only by their heads, but by their hearts, and all the assistance of the heavens. Because of the full connection this house has with them, it will probably suit them well.

The one Mr and Mrs Blarney eventually choose will fit their logic, and will probably support them in continuing to live in this limited way. Mr and Mrs Blarney will not change their circumstances until their heads tell them to. They do not believe there is any other governing force. Thus will their progress be impeded, until they realize there is more to the story of life on your earth; or until a wake-up call hits them.

Mr and Mrs Lark, knowing and trusting in a dynamic flow of life, of which they form a part, will be open to signs for changes needed and for clues on how and when. They will thus be flowing with their lives and the governing forces, and will be able to grow and experience much. Strangely, although it seems they have less direct control over events, they will probably feel more secure than the Blarneys, who assume they are following a tried, safe and sensible method. The Blarneys' security is brittle and breakable; the Larks' is as flexible as water.

Flow

In all your decisions and changes, you have this choice. Go by your head or by your heart and intuition; flow or try to control the flow. The problem with the latter technique, is that the flow is not ultimately controllable. You can only dam up water for so long, before the dam bursts, a leak develops or a floodgate must be opened. This is where the lack of safety with this 'deliberate method' enters. It is not that the Blarneys have no intuition. It is that they are denying it access to their lives. It is not that they have no hearts; but instead they are choosing to listen to their heads. The problem is that those parts of you which are denied eventually pop out somewhere, often when they are least welcome, and may cause the most ruckus. So Mr Blarney has a heart attack. This slows him down, opens him to his feelings and at last he starts to listen to his heart. Mrs Blarney gets depressed, and becomes incapable of thinking straight, which leads her to confront her feelings and eventually listen to them more.

Meanwhile Mr and Mrs Lark glide on through life, moving with the moment, and not needing major lessons such as these.

Universal support

'It is not so simple' we hear you say. 'These people who float around, following their intuition are usually irresponsible. They are not planning ahead.' You are absolutely correct. They are recognising that they are not fully responsible for the patterns of their world, and, in not fixing their plans, they are allowing the bigger and better plan to emerge. This does often confuse those around, who do not understand. But what better way to live could there be, than with the support of the universe? The support of one's own personal diary-organiser, even if it is in a classy gold-edged, black leather holder or on the latest iphone model, is not going to be quite as powerful! Living the Larks' way does not mean abdicating responsibility fully. Of course you still have to be alert for clues, be wary of false interpretations, and make the final decisions. The key difference is that you are not assuming you are the sole provider of information and opportunity. It is more like teamwork, which is closer to the reality of your world. None of you are islands, so behaving as though you are goes against the natural flow. You are all interlinked with so many realms and forces, so it is wise to include their offerings in your equation.

We have a little update for you on your friends. Mr Blarney recovered well from his heart attack, and, after a while at home, in which he became quite introspective and more feeling, he returned to work. His personal organiser became chock-a-block again, his head equally so, and Mrs Blarney, who had thought she might have a real live husband there for a while, found herself again living with a tired head. Her depression returned. Mr Blarney soon had a fatal heart attack. Mrs Blarney, shocked into her heart by grief, went to live with her daughter's family, where the lively voices of the grandchildren cheered her.

Mr and Mrs Lark separated amicably after two years in their new house. He wanted to explore the world, whereas she wanted to develop her career. They both felt they had learnt much from their relationship, and that it was time to move on. Mr Lark is now happy in Ethiopia, teaching; and Mrs Lark is now remarried with twins. She thinks she may return to her career later, but if that doesn't happen, she won't mind.

So, friends, the choice is always yours. Travel on your own, or invite the universe to join you on the journey.

The power of gratitude

Gratitude is a wonderful and undervalued phenomenon. If mankind realised what the effect of gratitude was, he would choose to experience it more often. It is not just another nice emotion, as most of you believe it to be. It is a powerful equaliser and creator of balance and harmony – reminiscent of the '=' sign in mathematics.

It is time you understood what gratitude is really about.

Energy loops

Imagine a loop of energy. It heads one way, turns and heads back to complete the circle. Now in your world loops of energy abound, on grand scales and on infinitesimal ones. Depending on what these loops are made of, what they are fuelled by, and what they are accomplishing, the quality of energy may diminish between the start and the finish of the loop. For instance, picture a relationship between two people. Person A does something generous for person B, who does not particularly appreciate this act of kindness. The energy of generosity from person A, strong initially, is given no reinforcement by a reciprocal energy from person B, and so begins to weaken. The energy at the end of the loop is more fragile than it was at the outset. An imbalance of exchange has been created, which person A will seek to rectify by being less generous next time. If person B had felt appreciation and gratitude, this energy would have fed the loop, so that it ended up being as strong at the end as it was at the beginning. This would have several effects. Not only is person A likely to continue the pattern of generosity, but person B is likely to do the same. The exchange between them is likely to be in balance.

This example is on a person to person scale. The same holds true on a nation to nation one, and in man's relationship to nature, space, his own body and all other matter. Gratitude has a close relationship to love, which orders all matter.

Gratitude strengthens

Gratitude actually serves to strengthen its object. In other words, if you feel a sense of gratitude towards nature, you are strengthening the energy of nature, by sending it love. You are also strengthening your connection with it, and ultimately, you are strengthening yourself, through that connection. If you feel gratitude towards a person, you are strengthening not only the person, but your connection, and yourself.

So, you ask, is it safer not to feel gratitude towards

someone you don't want to be connected to? No, it does not work like this. The connection we speak of is not like a friendship. It may not be seen or spoken. It is an energetic thing. As we have said, any true connection, connects the participants back to the source. Let us think for a moment of that energy of the loop we spoke of. Where does it originate? There is only one ultimate source of energy. This energy is then channelled by the person whose will and intent collect it for a particular purpose. The person then transmutes it into speech, thought or action. In sending gratitude back along the loop, you are connecting yourself with this loop, with its source and the person who channelled it. In allowing the loop to reach you, but not interacting with it, for instance in the case of ignoring someone's speech, you are denying yourself a potential connection with your source of energy.

The boomerang effect

There are of course many other possibilities of response, besides gratitude. Some of them actually serve to disconnect, or to otherwise damage or distort your connections.

However, we are discussing gratitude specifically here. It is not so much an emotion as a state of awareness of the order of things. In being aware of the implicit beauty of the order of things, you are reinforcing this order. You know this is how it works, as you know attention reinforces. But it is more complex that simply this. When you admire the grandeur of a mountain, you reinforce that grandeur, not only within the mountain, but within yourself. What you put out comes bouncing back to you. When you are grateful for someone's helpfulness towards you, you reinforce their helpfulness and your own. When someone is helpful to you and you fail to recognise this, you miss out on these benefits.

On a national scale it naturally works the same way. When a wealthy nation uses a poor nation, say in industry, and fails to appreciate the poor nation's contribution, not only is the connection between them weakened and thrown out of balance, but each of them is impoverished to some extent. If one nation appreciates the offerings of another, both benefit. If man has gratitude towards nature, both benefit.

Gratitude versus materialism

We see this on an energetic level, and it is a powerful dynamic indeed – one we wish you could see too. Gratitude and appreciation are tools for change and growth, which go unrecognised in your materially oriented world. As we see it, their effect on your matter is enormous. This effect is not made by words, such as 'Thank you', but by feelings that reside in the heart. Gratitude must be a genuine feeling, to have effect. It cannot be logically produced or guiltily manufactured by 'shoulds'. It must spring up of its own accord. It is a warm, expansive feeling, with a tinge of wonder and awe.

Gratitude tends to be smothered in those who place all their value on the material, and have much of what they desire already. It is hard for these souls to connect both with gratitude and with their own selves. The kind of feeling they often substitute for gratitude, on receiving more of what they desire, is a temporary elation, caused by distraction, fulfilment of perceived needs, and a short-lived sense of security. This does not have the same benefits as genuine gratitude. Instead of leading to connection, it tends to lead to addiction to itself. A cycle of greed is set up, to try to recapture this fleeting elation, and the longer the cycle continues, the further the person slips from being able to access real gratitude. It is a sorry cycle, and one that often necessitates an eventual crash, to awaken the victim to other opportunities.

Delight in the mundane

So, for yourselves, others and the world, seek opportunities to exercise your gratitude. It, too is a little addictive, as it makes you happy. Once you start noticing what life is offering you, and feeling appreciation, you will feel a degree of upliftment from the mundane aspects of your life. There is much to be noticed, and much to be grateful for. We would not have you all turn into grinning Pollyannas, but something between this and taking life for granted would be helpful, for all of us. Taking life for granted is a good recipe for brewing depression – it removes much of the magic from your every day. Once you start appreciating life for the amazing gifts it offers you, in the form of other people, places and experiences, the magic is put back in, with the twinkle in your eye.

CHAPTER 25

Laying the Foundation

Before you build upwards, you build a foundation which goes downwards, into the earth, for stability. This will serve to counteract destabilising forces, act as an anchor, and be the basis of whatever is built above. Should the foundation not be well constructed, the whole structure may collapse under pressure, or it may develop threatening cracks.

All the structures, endeavours and relationships you embark upon are equally in need of foundation. Unless they are firmly grounded, they may either not come to fruition, or might fail early on. Whether the project is your spiritual enrichment and connection, your job, a friendship, a hobby or the building of a boat, there must be a foundation of sorts, or it is unlikely the energy of it will carry it through to completion.

Left and right brain planning

Foundations may be built in various ways. They are often built through intent, in silence – the dreaming, planning stage. Sometimes they are built through actions which lead gradually to the desired result. They might be built through the left brain (logical thought, analysis, objectivity, and sequential planning), or through the right brain (dreaming, imagination, intuition, subjectivity and wholism). They will be most helpful and lasting if built through both. This is because neither, on its own, covers all necessary aspects. The left brain activity honours logic and linear process, but lacks laterality and creativity. The right brain has laterality, freedom and creativity, but does not necessarily have the stepping stones needed to adapt the dream to the 'real world'. Or should we say the 'unreal world' – the one of linear time, and sequential events, in which you choose to live. Or we could say the 'masculine world', for that is indeed what it is. So the more creative a plan it may be – the more right brain (feminine) activity it represents, the more left brain (masculine) activity will be needed to anchor it in life. This way balance will lead to strength, and the project will be self-sustaining.

You will have often seen the effects of a lack of this balance in the planning stage. People talk about others as being 'dreamers'. The 'dreamer' is seen to be someone who is full of ideas which are never actualized. The right brain is working overtime, but lacking support from the masculine side, which would provide the grounding needed for outward manifestation. Projects on a right-brain-only platform tend to remain in the ether only. Their would-be creators are sometimes labelled 'airy-fairy'.

On the other hand, you will have come across those who painfully process information through the filter of logic, carefully planning each stage, but missing the essence of the whole concept. The reductionistic approach of many of your sciences, illustrates this. Achievements built on this foundation may well manifest, but will be limited in imagination, due to the limited nature of the left brain's capacity for expanded vision. Any project built on a left-brain-only platform will not be whole. It will tend to be mechanistic and repetitive of existing projects.

So how to ensure you involve both sides in your endeavours?

Balancing reductionism and wholism

You have all enjoyed different experiences, through many life-times. For some of you the analysis of the left brain is anathema – whether male or female. You dance freely in the space of your minds and would feel utterly hemmed in by the structure thus imposed. For others the lack of boundaries of the right brain would indicate loss of control, and would be fearsome indeed. These ones cling to the rigidity, predictability and security of the left-brain processes, and we make no judgement on this. Preferences for different ways of thinking are as natural as preferences for different flavours of ice-cream. However, what we are trying to do here is show you ways of being which will help you in the long run. Should you always choose chocolate ice-cream, you may never come to discover how delicious the mango flavoured one is. Thus those airy-fairy-dearies who start to discipline their freedom just a tad, may actually gain the satisfaction of a project completed; and those left-brain-logicisers who step back to incorporate the whole picture, and who slow down to dream, may see their projects develop into wonders of imaginative creation.

A matter of scale

So, assuming the foundation is balanced in terms of the masculine and the feminine, what else is important? There is another simple law in terms of foundations. It concerns scale. The grander the project, the grander the foundation needs to be. A twenty-storey office block needs more than a two-metre-deep foundation. A doctoral thesis takes many months or years of research. A long-term relationship takes much building. A garden needs time to grow into maturity. A committee needs to get to know each other's styles before it can function maximally.

This is a matter of energy. The greater the energy expenditure, or exchange involved in the project, the more energy must be available to it from the start, for success. To explain this further: in the carrying out of a project, the energy that is expended must come from somewhere. Few people are well enough connected to their source of energy for it to be free-flowing. Therefore if a pool of energy is gathered, relative to the particular project, before it is begun, this will gradually feed the project during the building process. The 'builder' is then less likely to 'burn out', from feeding the project with his own energy. The more well-connected a person is to his source of energy and creativity, the less important this will be, as this person will seem to be self-sustaining. Energy will flow freely through him, as it is needed, to whatever projects he embarks upon. By now you can probably guess that we are going to advocate meditation or stillness as a prerequisite to the beginning of any new venture! This will help free up your connection to your energy source, so your project is well supplied.

Now let us return to the issue of scale. Obviously, if your project is the baking of a cake, you will not need to meditate on it. Paging through the recipe book and finding the ingredients will probably provide enough foundation for such an activity. However, if you plan to climb Mount Everest, not only will the physical preparation involve much effort, but the mental and emotional one may also. You will need to be sure you have enough mental stamina and emotional toughness in addition to physical fitness, supplies and supports. You will need a hefty foundation for this hefty project.

Thus if you seek to become closer to your soul, enriched in your life, purposeful in your direction, do not expect to achieve these overnight. They involve preparation of many kinds. A weekend course is not normally equivalent to the foundation for a lifetime's fulfilment. Let us imagine the foundation must be a tenth of the height of the outer building. This would mean, perhaps, that if we seek forty years' worth of fulfilment, we will need to put in four solid years' worth of preparation for this. Of course these are ludicrous figures, but perhaps they convey our meaning.

No magic bullet

Hence we would suggest that the overnight spiritual awakenings and conversions do not count for much in the long run. They may be the beginning of the preparation stage, but this is as far as they go. Sometimes they come at the end of the foundation stage, but more often at the beginning, when they give birth to many false starts. These well-meaning individuals may believe they have 'found it', and are now 'on the path', when, in fact, they have only just discovered there is a path, and must still find their way to and along it. Many disappointments and hitches often lie in wait for these ones, who, expecting plain sailing, must now be tripped up to discover true awareness. So be cautious about any sudden leap of evolution that has not been gestated adequately.

Gestating privately

Another point about foundations is their intrinsic nature of privacy. They only belong to their owner, and to no-one else. It is no good saying to someone who is brewing something 'Well, how is it going?' For they often do not know. It is a private and delicate process, this foundation-building, and must take its indeterminate time. If the builder is sensitive to his own needs, he will know when this phase has completed itself and the building is ready to begin. If he is not, he may either get stuck at this stage and never move on, but mull over and over; or he may get stuck into the next phase too soon, causing frailness or collapse of the project. It is a matter, ideally, of intuition and sensing, of knowing what feels right, ready and complete.

Clearing the grounds

Of course, before new buildings are built, the land must be cleared of previous buildings and debris. This must happen before the foundation is even marked out on the ground. Otherwise the foundation may be laid askew. Enthusiasm can often wipe out this important step, in its rush to 'get on with it.' The cost of this deficiency may be great. Projects built upon obsolete foundations will soon be obsolete themselves; and those built upon the remnants of past memories will be forever skewed towards these memories instead of being freely responsive to the moment.

So before embarking on anything of importance, clear the way and build balanced, proportionate foundations. Then you will be more likely to witness the fruits of your labours.

CHAPTER 26

The Sanctity of Life

Along your pathway to wisdom, you might eventually stumble upon a sign which proclaims that everything is sacred. This will be a sign worth reading and pondering on. There is not one grain of sand or flower petal, plastic bag or chair, which is not sacred. This is because they all originated from one source, and are all interlinked, back to that same source. There is not one object or life form on your earth, or in the whole of creation, which is not part of this connection. Therefore each thing you perceive, each quality you bring to bear upon the world, each statement you make is ultimately sacred. It is a reiteration of the creator who founded everything.

Perfection and experience

The implications of this realization are multiple. For one thing, judgement is displaced, once you understand the sanctity and therefore perfection of everything. Then, if everything is perfect, what is there to be done? 'Surely that must be the end of the story?' you ask, 'for what is the point of meddling with perfection?'. No, this is not so. For within the perfection is the pattern of experience. Without this pattern, the wholeness of creation would be severely dented, for this was the purpose of its design. The whole thing was an experiment, in a sense – an experiment which would be dynamic, experiential and free-flowing. So, by assuming all is perfect, therefore there is no point in doing anything, you are missing the point indeed. Part of the experience is for you to find meaning – be it short or long-term – and to follow this meaning to wherever it takes you.

Macrocosm and microcosm

The greater whole is in perfection – all the imbalances of your world are contained within this ultimately perfect resolution. There is the microcosm and the macrocosm. You could say the macrocosm is built of infinite numbers of microcosms. The macrocosm is always in balance and perfection. However the microcosms – the worlds within the worlds, though they are reflections of the macrocosm, may individually contain many imbalances. Compare this idea to the somewhat facetious idea that a family's weight tends to remain constant. When one puts on weight, another loses it, including the family pets. So while individual family members might be under or over weight, the family's joint weight remains the same.

Balance fosters evolution of the whole

It is thus with the perfection of your world. Ultimately, in the grand scheme of things, all is always in order. But look at one section under the microscope, and there are elements of dysfunction and imbalance, which may be rectified. Going back to the family analogy, you wonder if, when one area is re-balanced, that imbalance will then surface somewhere else. Not usually. Instead the process which may be enhanced is evolution. With enough balancing of the microcosms, the macrocosm, within its perfection, may be changed. There is not only one kind of perfection, after all. How many perfect sunsets have you witnessed, yet they were all different. Perfection, like all else in your world, is dynamic. Remember, each microcosm is a macrocosm for infinite microcosms, and so it goes on, endlessly. So, nothing you do is pointless. All attempts at balance affect the whole in its perfection, and are not wasted. All experiences alter the pattern. Those which create imbalance then foster further imbalance to correct this.

So the sanctity of all life does not mean leave well alone! It invites interaction, with respect. Interaction without respect is usually the creator of imbalance, which is a valid part of creation too, but tends to create suffering as a by-product. Suffering, too is part of the perfection of the greater whole, but it does not need to be so, and with enough evolution will become obsolete.

Honouring the sacred

The sacredness of all things demands recognition in your world. When it is not recognised, things go wrong. The older cultures on earth had a firm grasp on the relevance of these concepts, and knew the importance of honouring their environment and companions on it. If they honoured these outer manifestations, they were also honouring their own sacred connections. This meant they and what they related to were all firmly connected to the web of creativity, and they could manifest what they needed. This system of harmony was disrupted by the entry of competition and domination, which necessitated defence and warfare. Defence and warfare are alien to harmony and connection, so the links for these ancient wise ones were severed, and the patterns since have not allowed their mending.

Sacredness is not thought by the head. It is felt in the heart and in all the cells. It is an experience, not a thought. You do not have to go into the wilderness to access it. You can access it in moments of silence, in watching nature, in slowing right down to witness the patterns and the order in the chaos; in allowing yourself the awareness that you are part of all around you. It is recognition of your connection with everything, and of the validity of everything. You will know it when you feel it – it is a humbling, deep, quiet feeling.

So, if you wish to foster the evolution of your world, into one in which there is more harmony and less suffering, respect the sanctity of the earth and all upon her. Be aware of your connection to all people and all matter, and be aware of your connection to your source. If you manage to do these things, it is unlikely you will be motivated to cause any further imbalances on your planet, or in your small daily world. Daily sacred rituals may help remind you of these connections, but they will not replace your intent. It will not help you to read a book, choose a ritual and do it twice daily, unless your full intent and heart go with it. Then there will be some power to fuel the ritual, and it will help strengthen your conscious connections.

The sanctity of life is a beautiful thing. It is the secret ingredient which puts the beauty in nature, in art, in anything exquisite. Disconnect these from the source of life and they would not exist, let alone have beauty.

CHAPTER 27

Beyond the Worlds

Now is the time to contemplate. Your soul will be full of ideas about what you might do in the current and coming times. They will all be relevant. Your soul comes in with an agenda, unlike your personality, which is mostly built as you go along. Your soul's agenda is what will decide your future in the coming times. In the past you have been able to delay the dictates of your soul, through your personality, desires and ego. This is coming to an end. Soon you will no longer have that choice. You will be drawn willy-nilly to your soul's destiny. Whether you go kicking and screaming, or dancing and laughing, is the choice you have.

Completing agendas

There are worlds within worlds, and worlds beyond worlds. Somewhere is the place where your soul belongs, and where it will soon be, to act out its remaining play. Your soul may have a different destination from that of your loved ones. Or you may all be destined to go to the same place. This will be decided by the frequency your soul is destined to resonate to. Whatever is the case, this is the time to complete all the agendas remaining open, to complete all the businesses which are unfinished. There will be no mobile phones and emails in these worlds, friends, so communicate across the frequencies while you can. This will help free you up, and release you from frequencies you no longer need to be affected by. Let your history drop away, freeing you from heaviness and taking you towards light. The world beyond, where you are destined for, will not take your history into account. Where you were born, what you earned, what qualifications you had – all will not count for much where you are going. So hold these lightly, while you still need them, and do not define yourself by them. They are not you.

The reliable core

In the scheme of things, there is nothing more important in these days than your own connection with your innermost world. This is something that is permanent, reliable, and always calm, even in the midst of chaos. This core you have is the gem of your being – the essence of your infinity. It remains unaffected by all that happens on the outside.

Use this quiet centre to guide you through difficult times. Do not follow the dictates of your emotions, which can lead you far astray in times of crisis. Allow the experience and expression, yes, then move back to the centre, where all is in balance, and wisdom resides. Within the calm centre, you will find a joy, even in the most turbulent times. This does not mean you are out of touch with what is going on, rather that you are in touch with the infinite rather than the temporary.

Situations and states will come and go. You always have the choice: to be caught up in the drama of it all; or to focus on balance, peace and love. 'Oh!' you say 'How could I feel peace, when others around me are suffering?' What is the point of doing otherwise, we would ask? By all means, suffer with them, comfort them by resonating with them for a while. But if this carries on, you may all go into a downward spiral, and lose yourselves. So after a short time, elevate yourself back to calm. Imagine that you are all in a small boat. One person stands up, rocking the boat dangerously. The only way to correct this imbalance is to be extra still, until the boat settles down. If you all stand up, you will probably all fall in the water!

So do not get pulled and pushed around by theories, the media, politics and all the other external distractions you have so nicely created as a part of your entertainment. Be clear on who you are and where your soul is headed. Be open to ways of connecting with your inner being which feel right to you.

You are loved

Beyond this we would ask that you try to feel loved at all times, as you surely are. For there are countless of us caring for and about you in realms beyond yours. If you were the only human left on earth, you would be in good company. So remember this when times get tough, as they may. Call upon us, and ask for our help, and it will be given. This does not necessarily mean getting what you want. It may merely mean comfort or an easier trip. For sometimes your soul will have asked to go through certain experiences, and we would not deprive you of this.

Forever we will be in your debt. You who are human have forged a great part of the experiment of which we are all a part. You have added many new dimensions to the experience.

Now is a time for you to add another new dimension. It will be like changing your clothes in mid-air, as you jump from one space to another.

Preparing for the jump

How best to prepare for such a radical change? We would say it might be an idea to ensure you are wearing nothing to start with. That should make the process easier! If you have to both shed clothes and jump at once, you might fall short of the mark. So rid yourself of any extraneous baggage now, while it is still easy. That baggage may be in your thoughts, your emotions, your body, your relationships, or your personality. Whatever is not truly you – get rid of it now, so your jump may be unfettered. That may mean looking very carefully into that mirror we spoke of, and looking at the image behind the image. Expect the world within you to be a mini-version of the one outside. As you know, this is how it works. So examine your outer world with the scrutiny of a scientist:

- What sorts of things are happening to you?

- How do people relate to you?

- Does the world look exciting or frightening?

- If these are reflecting your inner world, what does this mean?

- What needs putting right and what needs celebrating?

- Do the lights always turn red just as you approach? Could this mean you are blocking your soul's path somehow?

- Do many people cheat you? How are you cheating your own soul?

- Are you bored at work? What makes you choose boredom above risk?

Shatter your own illusions, so you do not have to carry them, as their vibration may not allow you entry to paradise.

Finding your essence

So, friends, those who are paging their way through this book, who are you? If you still do not know, it is time for some serious stopping. Stop the emotions, the fidgets, the thinking, the phone scrolling and the television-watching, and be still. Just be still. That is the ultimate key to finding out who you are. Be still, and then be still some more. Into that stillness will eventually creep the essence of yourself, in the absence of anything else. Be ready to feel it, for it is quiet and not showy. It does not present as one of those larger-than-life advertisements, which you are all so used to. It is felt as a deeper stillness in the midst of your outer stillness. If you move, worry or look at the time, you may miss it. It has no agenda to be centre stage, so if you want it to be felt, you will need to invite it and make it welcome. The more that essence – who you are – is present on your stage, the less you will need other things, and the more contented you will feel. You already have nirvana. You just keep being too busy to remember that.

Loving yourself

Allow yourself the privilege of being understood by yourself. With self-understanding, you are likely to be able to love yourself. And if you love yourself, you're in the love vibration. It's a good loop to be in, if you want to access paradise. After all, who are you besides a spark of life, of conscious awareness? So if you love yourself you are loving that ocean of consciousness of which you are a part, and this is one crucial step towards being in sync with your soul.

Gravity is changing

Then there is the issue of gravity – yours and the earth's. Gravity is the pull exerted towards earth, as you know. It is responsible for many of your woes, like falling on your nose as a toddler and dropping eggs on your kitchen floor. However, it is also responsible for bringing you home. If you had no gravity, you would sail up into the air like a kite. Now, at this time in your history, your earth's gravity is changing. This is due to a number of factors, one of which is the polar shifts, another of which is the vibrational changes happening. Your earth is linked through a subtle network of energy, to all the planets, stars and other heavenly bodies. This is part of the reason for the coming change. It also means the coming change will impact upon a far wider community than yours. We cannot tell you exactly what to expect, for the gravity of the gravity change (sorry!) is yet to be determined. That is partly dependent upon how much of your baggage you sort out before the time comes. The more cleaning of garbage there is to be done on the part of the earth, the greater the shift will need to be. That much we can tell you.

Creating garbage

Look at it like this: You go to work on a sunny morning. You shout at your secretary, you swear at the fax machine for jamming, you curse God for stubbing your toe at the photo-copier. On the way home you do not see the blue in the sky, because your personal view has been clouded by your 'bad mood' i.e. your lack of clarity and mismanagement of emotion. You leave behind you all sorts of negative, heavy vibrations which your poor secretary, fax machine and photocopier are trying to incorporate or deal with. Because you are still clouded, and like attracts like, the neighbour's dog runs out and nips your leg as you fish in the letter-box. It's a bad day for you, and you have succeeded in amassing heaps of garbage for the atmosphere and your own consciousness to sort out. If this is becomes a pattern, it may be that the secretary will leave, the fax and photocopier will go on strike and you will get sued for kicking the neighbour's dog. Your wife may well decide she doesn't like that black cloud entering the front door, and leave also, or she may develop vibrations to match your own – not a pretty thought, indeed. We are being a little facetious, but what we are trying to say is that the greater the pile of rubbish, the bigger the clean-up and its effects will have to be.

Cleaning up

So it is indeed time for the great clean-up in your own small world. Do whatever you need to do to lighten yourself. Throw out those old assumptions, which have never worked anyway; toss away the expectations, of yourself and of others; purge the old judgements; sweeten the bitterness; farewell the disappointments. Clear your environment of unnecessary clutter – someone else probably needs it. Decide to stop wallowing in whatever has been your favourite emotion – move back to calmness. You will need it.

The garbage bin of humanity is already overflowing. Don't add to it by buying unnecessary chemicals, plastics, advertising slogans, gadgets, pressure to conform, to compete and to ride over others up the ladder of 'success'. Be yourself.

CHAPTER 28

Inner and Outer Space

Before you venture out onto the road alone, you look left, then right, then left again – or so you were taught. And many of you have followed this maxim ever since. A little caution is a wise thing. But too much caution is stifling. If you always wait at the crossing until the pedestrian light is green, even when the road is empty, you are wasting time and initiative.

The interaction of your inner space with the outer space of your world, is what we will attempt to address in this chapter. This is a delicate dance, and one that is handled uniquely by each person on earth. On the inside you are made up of a myriad of beings. Each archetype has its place within your personality, unconscious, memory, conscience and so on. Their interaction is another complex story. These parts of you work in concert, and in relationship to your soul, to create the person you find yourself to be. The only way you really find out the person you are, is by relating to the world around you. Otherwise it is only theory. So we imagine all the little people in you, enclosed in your skin, and reaching out to make their collective mark on the world around. This is where it gets interesting.

You are infinite

For the mark you make, in a sense, then defines who you are to yourself and others. Yet you have the choice to make millions of different marks, and each would be as much you as the others. So what does this mean? It means you are infinite, yet you define yourselves as limited, because the method of definition is faulty. How can you define an artist by one of her paintings, when her style varies greatly? When she does a still life you call her a still life artist. When she paints a mural you call her a mural painter. When she follows impressionist techniques you call her an impressionist. She is, in fact all of these and none of these. For she can do anything at all. What she decides to do is what the contents of her skin end up doing, but that is not all she can do, and certainly doesn't define who she is!

You are all inner space relating to outer space. And outer space relating to inner space. That is who you are, according to one definition. The truth is, you cannot be defined, in any other than a somewhat limiting way. The only real definition would say that 'you are.'

So we will look at the issue of your inner and outer space, without using it as a definition of you. How the two relate is what is of interest here, for there is an infinite choice of relationships.

Your management team

Within your bag of skin we have multiple beings, with a management team consisting of will, ego, soul and others. This management team will orchestrate the performance the others create in the outer world. If soul is the managing director, the performance will tend to foster spiritual growth, with other concomitants; if ego is the managing director, the performance will tend to foster image and status in the outer world. The strength of will dictates how well these goals are achieved.

Remember, though, there are two parts to the equation of interaction. There is you, and there is the outer world which will receive your mark upon it. The outer world consists of a busy environment with many other bags of skin in it, each making their marks in various ways.

Conflicting goals

Let us imagine that you have decided, after consultation between all your inner parts, to paint a wall blue. You reach out to outer space, buy the paint and get busy. But then someone else comes along who has decided in his wisdom, that the wall would best be yellow. Here is problem number one. It is called conflict. Now the conflict is between the two goals, you will have noticed, not the two people. The people are rather similar – both bags of well-inhabited skin, with ideas of how to make their mark. However, the yellow and blue paint do not have much to say to each other, so the two people find themselves interacting instead. You had decided on blue, and had put some time and effort into this decision – an investment, one might say. The other person had equally invested in yellow. Now what? We have one outer space, and two different marks wanting to be made upon it by two different inner spaces. Tricky indeed!

Stepping the dance

So this is where the dance begins. The quality of the dance will depend upon the dancers. There is no set outcome, and there are no set steps. Ultimately, in the scheme of things, whether the wall is blue or yellow, does not matter. It is the quality of the dance that matters, for it is this which will leave its mark upon your world in a deeper sense. Once these two people have moved out, someone else will come and paint the wall white, but the memory of the dance will linger on in the lives of the dancers, and possibly in the place. So choose your steps carefully, to make worthwhile memories.

Then there is the issue of conformity, once again. If one person chooses to forego his preference in favour of peace, this choice must run deep, or he is merely taking a toilet break from the dance, and it will continue in his being, causing rifts between parts of himself. These rifts are bound to spread one way or another, into the relationship eventually, to cause a new round of dancing – probably less pleasant than the first.

How to honour all choices? To honour means to listen to, to respect and to consider, not necessarily to adopt. All choices cannot be adopted, as some of them will run contrary to each other. However, many of the teams in the bags of skin will come to willingly change their preferences, once they know what they prefer has been given due consideration. They will tend to 'stick to their guns' more fiercely if not listened to adequately, as it seems to them their side of the argument has not received due attention, and must be better represented. So dance with respect and open ears.

It is too, a matter of choice. Do you choose to step lightly, or heavily? For that choice is always there. Do you choose to rest much upon this decision, to hugely value this mark you want to make on the world, or to see it as a transitory experience which is ultimately of no crucial importance. For these attitudes will dictate the tone of the dance. If you perceive the whole thing as merely a part of the pattern of experience, you will be able to step more lightly and adroitly. If you invest much in the decision, your steps may be less adept, more weighed down. It may be harder to turn the corners. So to keep your perspective is helpful. Sometimes, indeed, it may seem a worthwhile crusade, and you may choose a strong and determined gait. But in most cases this is unnecessary, and much energy is wasted in this way.

The risks of compromise

Having danced away, we now have a yellow wall with blue skirting boards – some sort of compromise – and both bags of skin are happy enough. They have each made their mark. However, to what extent is each satisfied? This will determine the quality of the ensuing dances. For if one is left not satisfied, a flavour will carry over from his inner space to his outer space. There is a slight imbalance which must be rectified, and unless our unsatisfied friend is exceptionally enlightened, it will seek to be rectified within the relationship – outer space. If he is not exceptionally enlightened, and he seeks to rectify the balance within himself instead, this may lead to further imbalance. He may start to justify his lack of satisfaction by reducing his acceptance of his self- worth; or by brooding on injustice or the perceived shortcomings of his 'opponent'. None of these are going to help his inner space or his interaction with outer space.

Those people who feel badly done by in your world will make their mark. It may be done inadvertently through their own imbalance, or it may be done consciously in a spirit of vengeance or justice. So it is folly to assume that when one person gets his way, all is well for him. It seldom works like this, because you all need to make your marks upon the world in the ways you choose; and you all affect each other.

Stagnation

Now there are some who prefer to stay quietly within their bags of skin, making as few marks upon the world as possible. Making marks feels dangerous – it may not be good enough, may turn out to be on someone else's wall, may turn out to be too hard, or may lead to frightening success. Instead they look left, look right, look left, and cross, walking only, at the pedestrian crossing. Such people view change with trepidation and challenge with fear. So they get what they want, as you all tend to do. Lives of little change or challenge, and much routine. To many of you this would be excessively boring, however these frightened ones are not bored. They feel safer this way, and this is their prerogative indeed. They do not like the quickstep, so they should not have to dance it.

There are others of you living this way too, who are bored out of your minds. Boredom and stagnation are signs that something needs to be stirred. You who are bored are holding so many treasures within your bags of skin, which are not seeing the light of day! Why not take a risk and let them out? There is probably a wall somewhere especially waiting for you to make your mark upon it. Once you start to access what you have, you will find there is more, and more. You will suddenly notice that your staleness has left. You will also notice that you feel more like the amazing human you were destined to be.

CHAPTER 29

Whirlwinds

Sometimes, on your journey, you will find yourself suddenly caught in a whirlwind. A cross-current has swept you off your feet and is hurling you around in a most disorienting fashion. These are the times to be on your guard. They can be times of trauma or growth or both. When the whirlwind has finished with you, it may spew you back onto your feet ahead of where you were before, or behind. Or you may find yourself landing on your head in an unknown place.

Confusion and the unconscious

Whirlwinds are all those events which seem to deny you your usual responses, and which throw you into confusion and the unknown. While you are swirling in space, the contents of your unconscious are likely to come to the fore, making it even harder to know what is going on, and how to feel and act. Suddenly you feel awash in grief, but you don't know why; or feel a surge of inexplicable anger or hurt.

These times are an opportunity for a growth spurt, if handled well. While hurtling through the atmosphere of confusion, grasp whatever you can that is sure, even if it is only your name! You need an anchor in order to have some stability from which to manage the situation. Part of your anchor must be the knowledge that whatever is surfacing from the unconscious is doing so for a reason, and that reason is probably a clearing out of old garbage. So allow yourself to feel whatever comes up – give yourself time, space and understanding. The more you do this, the quicker these intruding emotions will be satisfied and leave you alone. Don't hold back tears; if you're angry, pound a cushion. Remember that these are only your emotions and are not to be dumped on anyone else. However they are valid and must be allowed their voice, then allowed to leave. Sometimes it is worth trying to understand what they are caused by, sometimes not. This is the main strategy for dealing with the unconscious making itself felt.

Unprecedented events

However, you are still left with the original whirlwind – whatever threw you into the chaos in the first place. This will usually be an event unlike one you have managed before. What makes it so difficult is that there is no precedent, so there seems to be nothing to go by. There is no established routine for dealing with such situations, so you cannot reach to the past for answers. The future is often one big question mark at these times, so that is not much help either. What are you left with to go by? Only your heart and your intuition. Heads are notoriously hopeless on these occasions – their knowledge is too limited. Intuition, however, can be relied upon. If listened to carefully, it is like the lantern in the storm. You cannot possibly know what to do, but your intuition can, through its connections and its way of bridging time and space. So, in the islands between dealing with your unconscious promptings, listen very quietly to what your intuition tells you to do. Then follow it.

Holding your power

It may be tempting to go to others, who are still on stable ground, and ask their advice, but they are not you. They do not know your whirlwind, why it has struck you, or where you are headed. They can only speak from within their experience, or, if you are lucky, from their intuition. It is easy to be led off course. It is easy to follow someone's advice to quickly accessed safe ground. But this may not be what you need. It may be comforting to them to feel they have 'helped' you, while in fact they are doing you a disservice, or rather, you are doing yourself one in giving away your power. Sometimes you may genuinely need outside help, but usually it is best if you can battle the storm alone, as it is your storm. That way you will reap the benefits. Sharing your feelings about your experience is not the same as following others' advice. This may be helpful, but it takes a skilled and wise listener not to offer advice, and a strong whirlwindee not to take it!

The gift and the challenge

Ultimately, it is only another experience, to add to your repertoire. But in the experience you may gain many new strengths and skills, especially if you do it alone.

Whirlwinds strike for a variety of reasons. Sometimes they come to provide a shortcut, when a developmental phase is urgently needed. Sometimes they come to break you loose from established stagnant patterns. Sometimes they come as eye-openers and alarm clocks to awaken. Sometimes they come to crack open frozen wastelands, so new seeds may sprout. Whatever the reason, they are by nature difficult to negotiate, and cause much shifting and dislocation. Depending on how the whirlwindee, who we will call Jim, handles the whirlwind, he may end up more or less connected to his soul. The aim of the whirlwind is to bring him closer to his soul. There are several ways in which Jim might succeed in mismanaging it to such an extent that he ends up further from his soul. Let us look at these so we are all forewarned and forearmed.

Detours to avoid

There are many blind alleys Jim may inadvertently head into. He may get sidetracked by the strength of the unconscious emotions surfacing, and incorporate them in his life with others, instead of dealing with them alone. Thus might he start an added problem in his relationships, which might then be compounded by guilt, and so it goes on. Poor old Jim may be facing a divorce court before you can say 'lawyer!' He might have caused so much ruckus that he never really dealt with the original whirlwind issue.

Then there is the 'poor me' alley. It is one of helplessness and hopelessness. If Jim starts to invest in the belief that he doesn't have the skills to handle his whirlwind, he might well go down this track. This track leads to depression faster than you can say 'doctor!' Again, the original cause will probably be blotted out in the ensuing symptoms. There is the 'follow your friend' alley. This is a comforting alley, but a blind one. It leads to dependence and detours faster than you can cry 'help!' There is the 'escape into the body' alley, when it all gets too hard. The whole whirlwind is pushed out of consciousness and into the poor body, which leads to sickness faster than you can reach an aspirin out of the bathroom cupboard. And there is the blame response – 'it's your fault I'm in this pickle'. This is a good way to lose friends and avoid any growth. Some people even try to escape the whirlwind by relocating. It tends to follow until addressed. Some seem to become addicted to the adrenalin rush of the whirlwind state, and create whirlwinds one after another, with hardly a gap between. They don't seem to benefit from them, or get to a state of resolution. These people identify themselves with the whirlwind, rather than the space between, and it is very difficult for them to see the wood for the trees – they are so busy going round and round. This provides them with an escape from pain they fear experiencing, but creates its own pain in the process, including loss of identity and focus. Others will try to avoid dealing with their own whirlwind by helping others with theirs. It's a vicarious way of managing – a distraction, which does not lead to growth, on anyone's part usually. Still others will desperately try the logical, cognitive way. They will try to think their way through unthinkable problems, often ending up with worse confusion plus a headache. At best, they will find some limited form of solution.

It is these blind alleys and where they lead, which make people assume whirlwinds are terrible. They do not need to be, although they are not easy.

This too shall pass

Flow with your whirlwind. Do not battle against it, or force yourself to find a solution. Your intuition will carry you to safe waters eventually, if you let it. As you flow, be aware of the strengths you are exercising. Congratulate yourself! Remember, the whirlwind always comes as a friend, to help you one way or another. Befriend it and work with it. Use whatever strengths and tricks you have to flow with it, and be kind to yourself, knowing it is not an easy process. Give yourself patience. Eventually you will wake up one day and realise your world has become calm again, the dust has left the air, and the sky is blue. And you will have climbed up a few more steps.

CHAPTER 30

Rebellion and Evolution

Never consider yourselves at risk from fate. Fate is not decreed by some outside force, but by you and your own soul. You are never whirled about by forces unknown, without much input into the direction yourself, though it may at times seem so. Therefore, do not let it be said that you are a victim of circumstance. Yes, there are certain changes happening globally, but you have, in a sense chosen them. You always form a part of the great web of life, and, as such, you are always a co- creator of its focus and direction.

Awesome power

It may seem to you as though the part you play in the vast whole is so infinitesimal that it is insignificant. This is not the case. Each part is significant. Within the whole, you have a specific role to play which is not duplicated anywhere. Your role is both unique and essential. Think of how many people you interact with – in a day, in a month, in a year. Each of these people is affected by the way you play out who you are. This effect ripples out a long way, to multitudes of people. Each of these people is playing a part in the decision-making of your world, and each of them has been influenced at some level by you.

So, yours is quite a responsibility. This responsibility is not one to be worn with the gravity of the hangman's noose around the neck. Rather wear it proudly and gladly as a symbol of your power in the world. It is to be worn as a celebration.

Many of you do not realize that to have this power is an awesome thing. You believe your influence extends only as far as your action or speech. If only you could see the ripples you make in the whole pattern of life, how far they extend and how much they shape creation. Every thought, every word has a huge effect. So choose carefully and wisely.

Now we would like to explain something to you about this power of yours, and its effect in your world.

The rebel and the conformer

Imagine that 100 people are heading towards a particular direction in the intent of your world. If you add your intent to theirs, it may not make much difference, as there is already a strong pattern, which you merely add to. If, however, you head towards a different intent, you will start a counter ripple. Because it differs in direction from the major flow, your intent will have a substantial effect. Picture a lake. A swan glides down onto the water, leaving a wake of rippling water. Another follows from the same direction. The wake deepens. Then a third swan flies in from the opposite direction. The wake of this bird stirs and disturbs the previously formed wakes completely. Water bounces every which way, as opposed to the neat waves there were before. That third bird has stirred up the water more than the other two.

What do we learn from this? That the rebel has more effect upon the world than the conformer. The significance of this fact is that, while most people are drowning in conformity, and upholding old status quo's, those who decide to do otherwise will make a big impact. Now obviously there are rebels and rebels. There are the ones who while away many hours recalling their antisocial deeds in prison. There are those who scoff and scorn, but have no clear intent other than to destroy credibility and organization. There are those who carry a grudge against societies' wrongs, and refuse to join them. And there are those who see another alternative which seems more sound, and aim for it.

We suggest most of these rebels do your world few favours, though they may well have much effect, especially in causing the formation and maintenance of your criminal justice and security codes and systems. Some of these rebels fulfil an educational role through your media; and some fill spaces in psychiatric hospitals and drug dependence units.

It is with the last group, who envision an alternative, that we now speak. Many of you dear readers belong in this category, or you would probably not have opened this book.

Looking after number one

Every time you uphold your vision of a more sound

alternative for your world, through your thought, action or speech, you are making big ripples in the status quo.

Before you go on a rampage of reform, we would caution you to look after yourselves. For you are the ones most likely to overlook your own needs in the struggle to 'change the world'. Remember, you can only produce balance in the external world, if you have it in your internal world.

Further to this point, it is not beyond us to support you in your rallies and efforts. For each action you take towards the conservation of light in your world, is multiplied a thousand fold by invisible helpers.

Whenever you are wanting to add to the light in your world, remember to first shine up your own, as you would not want to be 'using up' your supply. What you need to access is a constant connection, so that you are merely a channel, not a supplier. For this to happen, you need rest and time alone with yourself, to focus on your own needs and energy. This being the case, you will find you are quickly transported through levels of development and clarity to a level at which you are well-connected and, in a sense, self-generating.

Being "self-generating"

This is the position from which you can make a vast difference to your world. Once you have accessed the 'self-generating' level, you will find you no longer need as much of certain things as you used to. Sleep, food, entertainment all become less important, as your system is more self-sufficient. As with all energy-related goals, do not strive hard to attain this state, or you will block it. Rather allow it – give yourself the time and space for it to access you. The above-mentioned helpers from other realms will then be able to bring in what you need for your evolution.

Discernment and creation

So, now we have you nicely developed – balanced, self-sustaining and relaxed. What next? Obviously the next step is for the constructive rebel to be able to clearly distinguish illusion from reality. From this ability can grow a vision – perhaps of how to lead illusion to reality, or how to replace illusion with a new reality. This, then is the ultimate task of the rebel – to create the vision, then to implement it, despite the pull of conformity and the status quo.

This is not always an easy quest. In fact, it is usually fairly tricky, due to opposition and fear on the part of the representatives of the status quo. However, if the rebel is truly well-connected and self-sustaining, this will ultimately bother him little. He will be able to persevere in the face of multiple odds, with much help from above. However, the quest must be very carefully chosen, as one which is constructive and not destructive. There is indeed a place for destruction of old ways and attitudes, but this is not the best focus for our rebel. He will get further in his quest to change the status quo by offering a sound alternative. No-one likes to be torn down, but some may be willing to entertain alternate ideas. These ideas may have to do with any facet of your lives. Their content is, in a sense, unimportant. The important thing is that you, as a rebel, are following your soul's direction; and that you are creating ripples of evolution in your world.

CHAPTER 31

Confusing Conundrums

In your lives there may be times of confusion, when you seem to be placed in the middle of a riddle, to which there seems to be no answer. These, like the whirlpool times, are times of challenge. We, from our greater distance, see them differently from you, and would like to share our perspective with you, in the hopes it may help.

Conundrums in which you are not the main protagonist, are generally best left to those who are, to sort out. Otherwise this is called interference.

A puzzle is made of many pieces, some of which have become displaced, and must be reassembled to fit the whole. This whole is in fact always there – a template which may be followed in the re-assembly process. When solving a puzzle, there are, as usual, steps to be followed.

Solving a puzzle

Firstly you need to ascertain which pieces are already in their correct places, and which need to be shifted. This in itself can be quite an exercise, and is certainly best undertaken before severe confusion sets in. After that it may be too hard to see the wood for the trees! The correctly placed pieces may then be used as a reference point and an anchor of sureness in the uncertainty. The wrongly placed pieces must be put in the foreground of your attention, for these must be moved. Now this is where the method splits. You can choose one of two ways to proceed. If you have lost the box with the picture on it, you will focus on a particular piece, and search for its correct position, referring to the known anchor of correct pieces you already have. This is a test of patience, perception and perseverance, and with time, these qualities may be rewarded by success – the completion of the puzzle, and the clarity and explanation of the whole picture. The other way is to study the picture on the box, and according to this, place each piece in position to match. This is much easier, as your reference point is more complete.

Whatever the puzzle you find yourself in, the process will be the same. And so will the choice. You can get caught up in the minor details, blind to the whole picture until the end, or you can see the whole picture and arrange the details to fit within it.

The danger in the first method is that you may spend much time and effort, and eventually find your reassembly does not work. There is a little section which seems not to fit at all. The end result does not match the missing template, thus there are confusing loose ends, and a resultant lack of completion and satisfaction.

Let us look at an example. Miss Bligh wants a satisfying career but is confused. Does she choose one which will earn her lots of money; does she choose the one her parents and family think she should do, or does she follow her passion, which is neither of the above? This has had her head spinning for several years. She really doesn't know how to come to a decision. In the meantime she plods on at her current job, which satisfies none of these criteria. There are many 'if's' and 'but's' milling around in Miss Bligh's crowded head. At least the current job serves as some sort of distraction from these. And at night the television helps by fulfilling the same role. However Miss Bligh's discontent is palpable, as are her tiredness and headaches.

The sorting process

Can we help her to sort out her dilemma? Let's see. The first step is for her to understand what is the problem and what is part of the solution. Her restlessness is part of the solution, not part of the problem. It is a clue to her of where she fits in to the big picture of her life. The problem pieces of the puzzle, which will need some re-arranging, are her attitudes about what is important. It is a problem that part of her believes she must conform to what others want her to do. It is a problem that part of her considers monetary reward to be more important than passion. It is a problem that she is using distractions to further her procrastination. If Miss Bligh can learn to see herself as an astonishing, unique person who has a life of her own to engineer, in ways that can lead to intense satisfaction, she will be likely to set aside all dithering thoughts of conformity and financial insecurity, and start creating her destiny. She will have found her missing template – the picture on the cover of the puzzle box. However, as long as she does not understand the problem is her attitude, she will tend to be stuck, and moving the pieces around in her head. She will be moving the pieces trying to fit them to a template which does not exist in her world, so of course she will not find their places.

Finding the missing template

The key is to find the missing template – then all can become clear. Then it is obvious which pieces are out of step, and which are well-placed. How to find it? This is not always simple. It is a matter of creating space in the busy head, looking honestly, perceiving what works and what doesn't, and being open to having illusions shattered. Miss Bligh was eventually lucky, in that her liberated cousin Petra came to stay. Petra illustrated so much freedom and happiness to Miss Bligh, that she began to imagine herself like this, for the first time. Her strength and courage increased as her illusions of powerlessness faded, and she applied to do the course of her passions at last, despite the tutting of her family.

Sometimes finding the missing template necessitates total physical removal for a while – a change of scenery for more distance and a better view of the whole picture.

Usually this can be achieved through – you've guessed it – stillness. This is an effective way of creating distance between you and the confusion. Guided meditations are not going to do it. They impose yet another activity on the mind, pleasant though they may be. What you need here is space.

The journey to wholeness

The missing template is the greater story of your life. The big picture of who you are and where you are really going, which is much of what this book is about. The story of your life is not about temporary ego gratification, security building and pleasing others. It is about your journey into wholeness. As soon as you can see this clearly, the facets of your dilemma start to fall into place naturally. You will know that whatever leads you towards wholeness is the next step; and whatever fragments or diminishes you must be what you leave behind.

If Miss Bligh had decided to do the course which her parents wanted her to do, she would have been honouring them above her own soul. This may sound very noble, but it is not. In doing this she would have been creating a barrier between herself and them, for when you dishonour yourself, you are creating inner conflict, and what is inside must manifest outside too. Thus every time she was bored in a class, she would inwardly have felt resentment against her parents, and reinforced her own sense of lack of courage. She would have been shoving her passion down, as though it was a badly behaved dog. Passion is an energy, and energies can only transmute. They cannot disappear. Thus her passion, which would have been so well expressed in the career of her choice, instead must boil over now and then in anger, sadness or inappropriate love affairs. If lucky, she might find hobbies or relationships eventually in which she could express something of her passion, while being bored stiff at work.

If she had decided to choose a financially rewarding career, the results might have been rather similar, except perhaps she could afford more expensive trinkets and holidays to ameliorate her boredom.

Suiting yourself

When Miss Bligh chose to follow her passion, she found herself on a shortcut to her soul. The more she is who she is, the more her identity will unfold. The more she is not who she is, the more she identifies with who she is not, and the harder the way back to herself. That sounded like a conundrum in itself! But that part is really quite simple.

What may seem less simple is the puzzle in which you seem to have several equally appealing choices, all of which seem to suit your soul. How to place the puzzle pieces then? You can choose between parallel lives. Perhaps it doesn't matter which way you then choose, as each will offer its own experiences and growth. Or perhaps, if you listen for long enough, your intuition will whisper to you which route to take. Remember, as we have said before, there is no one right road for you. You design your life as you go along. It is just a matter of designing one which will suit the template of your soul.

CHAPTER 32

Mastery

Mastery over yourself is something you can all aspire to. It is no longer unattainable except to the few. Your world sorely needs masters now. The beauty of mastery is that it is like a breath of clean air in your world, untainted by all the chaos and pollution around. The master does not lean on society's structures or rely on others' norms and values. Instead he initiates his own structures or lack thereof, and designs his own architecture in which to live. This life then is a free one, unimposed upon by external factors, and supported by internal ones. This does not mean the master is selfish or irresponsible; a recluse or a misfit. On the contrary, he must be able to join in the game of society, but play it by his own rules, in order to qualify.

Masters and servants

The master sees the game and chooses with discretion how he will respond and play. The servant of society merely responds as a conditioned puppet of ego, fear and the status quo. There is a world of difference, even though they may both be playing the game. The master enjoys the game, able to dodge, step aside, duck, counter and learn from the rebuffs and challenges of the daily grind. The servant is in survival mode, and each challenge is a potential threat to well-being and life itself. He falls into the troughs, and bumps over the corrugations on his path; while the master somehow glides over them, not necessarily effortlessly, but effectively. The servant is pulled and pushed by the storms of the human world; is buffeted around until semi-conscious. The master allows himself a certain degree of pull and push from intuition, or higher forces, but ultimately decides on his direction through clear consciousness.

How to attain this dizzy height? There are many roads, as you know, but several tips hold good for any of the roads you may choose to embark upon. Let us discuss these.

Intuition versus gut feeling

You will have all heard plenty about intuition by now. Yet this topic has not yet been fully understood by most of you. Intuition is not just about listening to your 'gut feeling'. It is about far more than that. Your 'gut feeling' is to do with your own make-up, your response to inner and outer promptings. It is a valuable yardstick, but can be misleading, just as your feelings can. The unconscious can play tricks with the 'gut feeling'. Fears stored away down there can surface in the 'gut feeling', leading you astray. No, there is more to intuition than that. Intuition is about connecting with the absolute, with the higher part of yourself, which is tied in to your destiny. It is holding an earphone to the wire of true consciousness, while blocking out the ring of illusion. Intuition can pass you glimpses of the past and future; it can jump through space; it can give you understandings you never dreamed of. Intuition can bypass logic to solve insoluble problems and show you the unseeable. It can bypass beliefs and go straight on to knowledge. Intuition is the magic teacher, which most of you do not seek to learn from. This is often because you think you do not 'have it.' This is not true – you all have intuition. It is a given part of your tool kit as humans. But if you do not believe this you will not use it to your advantage. Intuition is very much like a muscle – it atrophies with disuse. Conversely, the more you use it, the stronger it becomes. Honour and trust your intuition and it will reward you with multiple blessings. Listen carefully to it, hear it well, and you will hear the voice of truth sounding in your heart. It may take a little practise to distinguish its voice from that of wishful thinking, fear or other of your daily companions, but, if you are keen to befriend it, your intuition will soon become your great ally.

Stillness invites wisdom

Another factor to take into account, if you aim to be a master, is stillness. We have mentioned this word again and again, perhaps because it is so important and so undervalued in your world. Stillness of mind and stillness of body form an invitation for wisdom and clarity. While all is whirling in the mind, how can any new information infiltrate? Stillness is an invitation to intuition, and to connections with higher realms. Set aside regular times for stillness. This is as important an activity as any other. Just because it appears you are not outwardly doing anything, do not undervalue the exercise. You are doing far more than you realise, at an energy level.

Cultivating oblivion

Then a master also needs oblivion. He needs to be able to focus so well that he can put all else out of his consciousness. He needs to be able to be oblivious to what is irrelevant for him. This means he is able to direct his attention and power to where it is meant to go, without diluting it on trifles. His task is the betterment or serving of his soul, and whatever serves this is the primary direction of his focus. This direction he will find in stillness. Distractions may be costly, and are best avoided. So a finely-honed and disciplined mind is a precious tool indeed. This can be attained through meditation practises of various sorts.

Lightness of being

No master would be worth his salt without humour of some sort, for humour is the reflection of the lightness of his being. Without it, he would be dour indeed, and no master. A master is defined partly by his ability to perceive life's anomalies as from a distance – a bird's eye view, as you say. From this distance, how could he fail to see the humour in it all? Humour is one of the colours of your human rainbow. It sits alongside pathos and balances many conditions. So, if you wish to become a master, cultivate your humour. Step aside, step beyond, and look afresh at life's pathos.

In its shadow, you will see the humour. There is no harm in this, you can respect both the pathos and the humour equally. They both have their place. You are not becoming flippant, but realistic. Of course we are not advocating laughter at the misfortunes or expense of others, but at the incongruities, the ironies and the surprises in life. There are plenty of these, and seeing their humour will help you and others to deal with them, and to remain light-hearted. Light-heartedness is a definite pre-requisite for a master.

Exercising courage

A master must have courage. Without courage he would not be able to confront his demons – those aspects of himself working against his best interests. Following your intuition will often entail exercising courage. The way to develop courage is to use it. The best environment to practise it in, is one in which you feel fear. Everyone has courage. That, too, is a tool you were all issued with. If your fear feels greater than your courage, you may be mistaken into believing you have no courage. That is never the case. In a situation such as this, a good trick is to act as if you had courage, then you will find you do have it.

Walking the webs of interaction

He who would become a master also needs friends. This is because he needs to interact with the world, and relationships are one way to do this. Through his relationships he can test and hone his mastery. Does this go contrary to what you thought: a master should be self-sufficient? As we see it, this is not so. For what is the point of being a master in splendid isolation? The point of being a master is surely to represent the state of freedom within and without. How can this be accomplished without the context of relationships? It can, but there would be huge components of competence missing. Within relationships, the master can fine-tune his ability to walk a balanced line along the webs of interaction, while contending with the range of emotions this entails. It is far easier to be an isolated hermit in a mountain cave, but far less rich an experience. Remember, what is delivered to you in relationships is a selection of mirrors of aspects of yourself. So, if you can accept and deal with these, you are achieving mastery over yourself. Besides all this, relationships can be most enjoyable, and there is no need for the most dedicated of would-be masters to deprive himself of enjoyment!

Time

To become a master you need time – time to reflect, time to ponder, time to be clear on direction and values, time to perceive what is going on around, time to let go of what is no longer needed, time to go with your own flow, at the right pace. This time must sometimes be consciously set aside, lest it all get swallowed by the great god Activity, who has an all too eager appetite. The time spent thus is a great investment indeed.

As you head on the road to mastery, spare a thought for those who have no idea of this concept. They may be following a different road, but theirs is as valid as yours. Your acceptance of them will be a test of your mastery.

CHAPTER 33

Small Steps

When crossing a stream on stepping stones, you have the choice of how big to make your steps. Do you stretch between each third stone or step gingerly on each one? The decision will dictate the size of your step. If you choose big steps, there will be fewer needed to reach the other side, but you might be more likely to fall in, as the stretching demands more balance. If you choose small steps it may be safer and slower, but will possibly be less exciting.

Choosing your pace

In designing your future, you will need to decide upon the pace which suits you personally. For many of you, small steps will be appropriate, as you will not be used to taking risks. It may also seem as though there is already so much change around you, that you want to slow it down, not speed it up. You may feel as though you are being led along at a pace which you have not chosen at all, but in fact, you will always be able to slow or speed up the pace, within the framework you find yourself in. This is because you will still have free will, and because time will become more flexible than your experience of it thus far.

The steps we are referring to here are the steps to the destiny you are currently creating. Take small ones and you will get there safely but more slowly; or take big ones and get there faster, but with greater risk of slipping along the way. The choice will always be yours. Each of you will find you are offered opportunities of big steps – shortcuts along the way. You will need to learn to tell if you are ready to take these or if you need to pass them by and take the slow route. You will need to discriminate carefully so you can pace yourselves. As time goes on discrimination will become easier for you, but until then, we advise short, safe steps for all but the most confident and adventurous. You have all been on those short-cuts which end up being long-cuts, have you not?

Being kind to yourself

So go easy on yourselves. Do not push yourselves into situations which seem too challenging, as there will be enough challenge in the changes around you to contend with. Your energy fields will be changing fast, and you will need to rest often and may feel tired and out of sorts. There will be many shifts within and without to adapt to. This is not to say you are not used to change. Of course it is the constant state of your being and your world. But here we are referring to an accelerated pace of change, and changes of frequencies, which affect the very fabric of your body and way of being. So drink lots of water – this will help you adapt – and take it easy.

You will later find you are able to make vast changes in your lives with little effort. It will seem simpler to decide. There will be fewer distractions and more clarity available to you. It will be a time of much movement and much growth.

Keeping focussed

During this time you will need to focus on your aim. It may be easy to let the pace of change carry you in directions you would not otherwise choose. So be discriminating about your goals and the direction in which to head. It may seem as though a world of possibilities is opening, and this may confound you and throw you into quite a spin. At these times ground yourself before you make any decisions. Let yourself come back to a sense of clarity and stability before you make the next move. You will have time to do this.

You will find it remarkable how quickly you can adapt to the changes you make. The old will seem to drop away from you with ease, and the new will become an almost instant part of your life. This will be due to a reduced collective resistance, and the higher frequencies at which you will be operating. It will seem as though you were always like this and you will strain to picture the slowness of the old ways of adapting to change.

Perceiving home

The changes of which we speak do not revolve as much around monetary and other systems as around personal interpretations and ways of perceiving. You will find that what seemed mysterious will become clear and what seemed clear may longer be so. Disillusionment, it is called, and awakening to reality. These new perceptions will in turn quickly lead to changes in your systems of organisation. Once humanity collectively sees what it is doing, it will change to far saner ways of operating.

There is no doubt that you will like what you see happening around you. It will feel as though you are all coming home. It will feel as though the jigsaw pieces of humanity are at last falling into their allotted places, and the picture is becoming visible. There will be a communal sense of relief, as of great weights falling off your shoulders. The accumulated clouds of centuries of illusion will at last melt into clarity. You will see each other for the first time, and may be quite astonished at what you find.

Multi-dimensional midwives

While this is taking place, there will be a wave of intervention from other realms, assuring that the changes taking place are steered as appropriately as possible towards peace for all concerned – and this means for more than just humanity. As you now know, there are many others affected by events on Earth, and during this time they will be there, determined to help mankind to make the most of this unique opportunity. There will be some determined to capitalise on the occasion purely for their own benefit, but they will stand little chance of success, as they will have little support.

CHAPTER 34

Revision Time

Before any birth there are pains - the pains of readiness for a new beginning. There will be a stretching, an opening, a bit of a squeeze, then new life begins. This is what you may all expect on Earth before long. There will come a time when you ask yourselves whether you are ready, individually and collectively for this great shift of consciousness. The answer will be different for each individual, but the process will be the same, for it will be a collective shift. For some it will seem like a small change, while for others it will be a leap unfathomably large. The end result will be the same for all - the ending of illusion and of the illusory world with all its systems of government, enslavement, forced obedience and collusion. Instead it will be the beginning of true freedom for all. This might sound impossible within your present framework of thought, but this too will be no more. Your minds will be shifted to another paradigm of ability, and you will know what to do and what your new choices may be.

Preparing the new paradigm

So until then, prepare yourselves for this new

reality, by stating clearly to yourselves what you would want in it and what you would rather leave behind in the "old world". For although it will seem to you as though this shift is imposed upon you, it is you collectively who are creating it, and it is you who must steer its creation as carefully as possible, especially at this crucial time. The energy for the shift has now built up to huge proportions, and what is left is for it to be clearly directed. Each one of you is a part of the collective, and each one of you therefore has power over the direction of your future. We have spelled this out for you many times, and we do so again: Do not waste this opportunity to create your destiny as you have never been able to before. You have, it is true, always created your destiny, but the power behind what you are doing now is unprecedented, and the distance between the points it could lead to is great. We know you will create paradise, as the channel for this has already been formed. It is how you get there that is the question.

Taking stock

We stand on your side-lines and we look with wonder at how you humans manage your world currently. It is a maze of contradictions to us. On one hand it seems there is so much order, on the other complete chaos. Within the chaos there are people scrambling to get out to calmer places, trying to catch their breath in a collective sigh of longing for something simpler. And within the order there is a rigidity which suffocates many who only want to understand how to be. We would advocate a sitting back on the haunches, for all humanity, and a taking stock. Until you can see where you are now, you will not be able to see the way ahead. For there is a way, waiting for you to stumble upon it. It is marked out in the ether, clearly in white chalk, as the lines on a football field. It is a way for all of you, which currently few of you can see or even imagine. But it is there.

It is the way of peace.

The way of peace

You have all spoken of peace, particularly during times of war, but few of you seem to understand how to attain it. There is actually an easy recipe for peace. It is about silence and going within. Once you have pulled all the stray ends of yourself inside and closed the shutters, you will find you can access all knowledge and all peace. This, we know, sounds simpler than it is for you to achieve. We look upon you and we see busy minds, flurried hands, darting eyes, feet moving this way and that, hurrying to get into the next future. Were we to stop the film and freeze it into a still picture, we would see each person caught in a position of frozen movement, stuck in time between yesterday and tomorrow. The Earth herself would hold her breath, supporting Man in his state of stasis. But we cannot do this, so instead we look at ways of creating a similar effect.

Life-changing happenings

One way is through happenings of huge importance to man – happenings which stop each person in her tracks, which make each person gasp, and be jerked out of the current reality and into a new position. These occurrences set the stage for a new perspective, for a sense of unity of the collective, for empathy and compassion, and for a retreat into contemplation. For a time they enable man to look further than usual – past his short-term goals and into the very heart of what it is to be human. While man is doing this, he is creating peace, for peace is made of contemplation not action. (We smiled at your peace marches, for they were a contradiction in terms, though the intent was useful and the result was beneficial.) While this contemplation takes place, there is a concurrent growth in man's soul. It is as though the much-neglected soul feels valued at last, and steps into the foreground to be seen. At these times there is much inspiration, and many new thoughts and new leaders emerge. And the messages from their souls are heard by many, feeding the souls of humanity collectively.

Blame and retribution

Now, during these times there is often another concurrent process at work, as you know. This is the response which hinges on blame and retribution; which declares war on peace. One of the reasons you have chosen to create this response among the minority is to highlight the importance of peace – to make peace an issue which is thrust into the foreground. For peace too easily becomes a background issue, taken for granted while apparently there, and soon diluted into a murky solution of troubled waters.

New priorities

So, in the past few years you have witnessed many shocking world events which have surprised you out of your complacency and turned you towards each other in horror, doubt, empathy and fear. After these events neighbours may speak to each other for the first time; people look at their living families in appreciation for the first time; and many for the first time give thanks for what they have. People take stock. And in the silence of their beds at night they take stock of themselves. Out of this stock-take comes a new reverence for life, very often, and a new sense of reality and priority. This is gradually turning your world towards its future.

New leaders, new discoveries

There may be power-hungry members of the human race at the helm, eager to use the rest of you for their own ends, but this will not be for long. For the collective shift is stronger than the weak power of these individuals, whose souls are not aligned with their wills. One by one you will see them crumble and quietly leave the stage. Then the stage will be set for new leaders, who will be very different. By this time humanity will well and truly know what it wants, and will be well equipped to create exactly this. So you will find there is a turning about of almost every system you have, as they are all currently unworkable in a long-term sense. There will be discovery upon discovery, of new ways to do things, of new ways to organise and manage and of new systems. Once the old leaders are gone, it will all move quite fast, as there will be little resistance to change.

New clarity

This is when each person will discover what their unique talents are, and how they fit into the whole. Currently only a few of you know these things, as there is so much distraction, mainly from competition and conformity. However at this future time of unfolding of your new world, these issues will no longer take centre stage, enabling clarity and individuality to emerge as never before.

So see this as a time of wonder, of waiting perhaps and certainly of planning. Become clear on your dissatisfactions with the current way of being, the current systems and expectations. Even if you cannot at this stage envision an alternative, know what you would want to leave behind and what you would want to take with you. Become clear on what feels right and what feels out of step with the future you would want. Give your soul plenty of opportunity to talk to you in silence, so world disasters do not need to be created. Gradually, while doing these things, you will be creating paradise.

So enter into this next phase of your collective journey with lightness of heart, for it will indeed be a time of wonder, discovery and excitement.